Birth of a White Nation

The Invention of White People and Its Relevance Today

Birth of a White Nation

The Invention of White People and Its Relevance Today

by

Jacqueline Battalora

Strategic Book Publishing and Rights Co.

Strategic Book Publishing and Rights Co.
12620 FM 1960, Suite A4-507
Houston TX 77065
www.sbpra.com

ISBN: 978-1-62212-722-1

For my family:

Diana Vallera and Francesca
My parents, John and Arleen Battalora, my sisters Terese and Mary, my brother David and my friend, Ricki LaFayette Brigham

Table of Contents

Acknowledgements

When I first identified myself, in a self-conscious way, as white, I was about thirteen years old and living in southern Texas. I had moments where I experienced my whiteness as something contingent upon behavior. I came to realize that a white racial status was something that could be changed, and perhaps even lost.

These were my earliest clues that the "white race" is not rooted in nature or the result of biology. These early experiences of race, combined with a heavy dose of Catholic social justice teachings (primarily expressed and encouraged by my mother, Arleen Battalora), significantly shaped my life and my studies.

While this book is steeped in history, law, and sociology, it is equally influenced by social ethics. This ethic has its roots in social justice teachings. I was fortunate to pursue undergraduate studies at Siena Heights University, where the faculty in the religious studies department, Susan Conley Weeks and Donna Kustusch, O.P., fostered critical thinking and introduced me to liberation theology through the writings of James H. Cone and Gustavo Gutierrez O.P., and the feminist critiques of Rosemary Radford Ruether. These "outsider" writers helped give greater substance to my white female experience by giving voice and legitimacy to the lives of those who were not white and/or not male. For this early fostering of critical thinking, especially within religion, I am indebted.

While my life experience of race shaped my academic interests, studying with Rosemary Ruether in graduate school at Northwestern University laid the foundation for this book. There I was introduced to the now-classic article on white privilege crafted by Peggy McIntosh, and to the writings of David Roediger, Noel Ignatiev, W.E.B. DuBois, Edmund S. Morgan, and Alexander Saxton. Joseph Barton helped guide me through what seemed a daunting historical record. Bernard Beck in the Sociology Department helped me love sociology. I continue to find the most fundamental tools of analysis within the discipline of sociology to be invaluable. Rosemary Ruether helped orchestrate my interdisciplinary interests throughout graduate studies at Northwestern and encouraged the pursuit of studies wherever they led, while also facilitating the completion of a dissertation. She remains my valued mentor, colleague, and friend.

I have been fortunate to have the input of valued colleagues and friends. Many read chapters and provided feedback. I especially thank Yulia Borisova and Rick Angell. They helped the first few chapters become more clear and readable. Eddie Moore, founder of the *White Privilege Conference*, has provided a platform for sharing and testing my work in the area of whiteness in relation to U.S. law and policy every year at the conference. I have benefited tremendously from these experiences and challenges. I am grateful to my editor, Jennifer Abel, whose editorial skills have improved the consistency and the clarity of the text.

I am grateful to the journal, *U.S. China Law Review* for permission to reprint sections of an article of mine previously published that appear in Chapter Three. The lynching images in the Afterward of this book are from the Allen/Littlefield Collection.

I am indebted to Saint Xavier University for supporting this research and writing through release time and an invaluable sabbatical. My students at Saint Xavier University have served as a testing ground for these writings. They have challenged my assumptions, helped clarify concepts in the dreaded theory section, and encouraged me beyond words. While I alone am responsible for shortcomings and errors in this text, I have largely my students to thank for whatever strengths and insights it offers.

Finally, I have my family to thank for supporting my work and studies in the areas of racial justice and white awareness. This work takes me away from them more than I would like, but sharing the value of its effort and intent makes it feel like a project that we share. My father, John Battalora, and my mother, Arleen Kann Battalora, supported me through my many years of labor on this project. While they have not always understood my stubborn focus on the topic of race (and especially whiteness), they have been a persistent positive influence and helped drive the publication of the work. Diana Vallera, my companion through life, has been my greatest cheerleader. Through her work as a union leader, I have marveled at her centered approach in the face of personal and institutional attacks. Almost daily, I draw strength and inspiration from her ability to endure adversity and stay guided by the basic needs of laborers and the principles of labor unity. Our daughter, Francesca, has kept me at ground level rooted in the moment. She has no idea how much she inspires me. She is a constant reminder of the human capacity to love and experience and express joy. She is also a reminder that both are expanded when shared.

On Autobiography and a Study of Race:
An Introduction

Any exploration of race is inherently complex, because personal experience cannot be erased. Every person is assigned a place within the racial landscape, and our experience of race shapes how we see what we see. In other words, life experiences are often very different depending upon one's race, and these experiences impact how we make sense of events. This is especially true when we examine race. Personal experience aside, a study of race is challenging because scholarship addressing key historical questions is varied, sometimes in opposition, and sometimes indeterminate. Furthermore, language of "race" is problematic and confusing. I will address each of these challenges before discussing the theoretical approach that will guide this study of race.

Comedian Steve Martin began the film *The Jerk* with the words, "I was born a poor black child." Laughter filled the theater as the audience stared at the image of the speaker, a very, very pale-skinned man familiar to most as the funny guy who frequently appeared on *The Tonight Show*. I have thought of that line, the audience's laughter, and the assumptions upon which the humor depends often as I have processed my own thinking about race. My first conceptualization of myself is that I was born a young white child. By this I mean that I saw myself as "white" and viewed it as an essential part of who I am, having a biological reality that links me to all others who are white through a shared genetic sludge that is "whiteness."

Now, I know better. Now I would say: I was born female and made a white girl. What has stayed consistent is that the status "white" has mattered in my life. My understanding of why it matters, though, has altered dramatically.

Birth of a White Nation

As I was undergoing these changes in self-concept and growing socio-historical understanding, I knew they were significant. I realized I would never be the same and neither would the world in which I inhabit, because my perception of it had changed. There was no going back. As a teacher, I have watched students undergo similar transformations and growing awareness. While teaching has many challenges and rewards, these "ah-ha" moments are some of the most gratifying. The compilation of laws, histories, and analysis within this text has been selected and organized to help foster such learning moments.

The primary concerns of this book are to uncover the social efforts deployed to create a racial category, to explore the ways in which the racial category "white" has become central to the organization of society, and to realize the consequences. I can claim no objective distance from the topics in this book: race, human division, social constructs, and the always-present intersections of race, class, gender, and sexuality. Indeed, my interest in these issues has grown out of my own experiences of them.

I spent almost the first decade of my life living mostly in Europe, until moving to a small city in southern Texas. Despite living in Europe, my family spent many weeks over the summers visiting my grandparents in the Chicago area. I did not realize it until much later, but those summers in Chicago constituted crash courses. Chicago is known not only as the Windy City, but as the southern city of the north. Summers in Chicago provided cultural familiarity for the future move to southern Texas. As it turns out, Corpus Christi, Texas is the windiest city in the U.S. Although, truth be told, the reference to the "windy city" came about not because of the cold winter gusts off of Lake Michigan that chill you to the bone, but rather because of how Chicagoans spoke (windy) about their city when it hosted the World's Columbian Exposition in 1893. It turns out that this proclivity toward windiness in reference to one's geographic location was also good training for a move to Texas. Texas fosters its own culture of wind about itself, in an aggrandizing way that is pervasive and unique, and no world's fair is required.

Those summers in Chicago first introduced me to a racial landscape that was the norm throughout the south. "White" people were in their own areas and "others," especially African Americans, were in theirs. Family and friends fled in the late 1960s from the Lithuanian neighborhood in Cicero that they called home. They left soon after African Americans began to exercise their rights to pursue home ownership where desired, rather than in the areas to which they were relegated by restrictive covenants and violent neighbors. My relatives who could afford to do so headed to a residential neighborhood in Arlington Heights, a northwest suburb of Chicago, where their neighbors, on the surface, looked like them.

The move to Texas brought into clear focus the divisions and separations I experienced in small bursts on those summer visits to Chicago. In Victoria, Texas, people lived in areas that reflected not only economic class but also the relative shade of one's skin. Railroad tracks literally and figuratively served as a significant human divide. Within two years, probably much less, I learned that separating the "races" was the culturally expected norm, especially in romantic relationships and particularly when a "white" woman was involved. As I grew up, I experienced race generally as something firm and unchanging and yet in certain moments, usually of strain, I experienced my "white" racial status as contingent on behavior consistent with the expectations of "whites." In these moments my race became palpable as something that can be lost or at least changed, creating the experience of race as something other than an immutable product of nature.

I cannot pretend to be uninfluenced by these experiences. They made me "white" even while presenting hints of its fictitious nature. Both the reality and fiction of whiteness co-existed in my experience and created the desire to make sense of that contradiction. This struggle helped give direction to my graduate studies. I enter into this project having first studied law and then sociology, U.S. history and social ethics in an interdisciplinary Ph.D. program. These academic disciplines shape the approach taken to the concerns addressed in this text.

I pursued the study of law because it was the most obvious avenue for engaging in efforts to improve the distribution of opportunity, access, and resources, liberty, rights, and freedom. However, law presented its own inequities that I struggled to sort and clarify. When a judge in a rape trial interpreted hands around a woman's neck as foreplay, thereby dismissing an alternative perspective (that those actions could reasonably be experienced as a threat of strangulation), it brought into focus a gap between my view of the world and that which was recognized in a court of law. There were many of these moments and I soon realized that, too often, my version of "reality" was not the authorized or legitimized version. I felt more and more distant from the world in which I lived, especially the "world" of law, because it is a significant legitimizing institution that often authorized a "truth" that was not mine. I pursued further graduate studies because the structures of "reality" and "common sense" that were simply taken for granted by legal actors did not fit my experience of reality, and I struggled for the words and concepts to name and explain this gap.

In many ways, this book is a result of that pursuit. Today, I still click off "Caucasian" or "white" among the "race" options on the census and those official forms at schools, medical providers, etc. What is different is that today, I know that "white," like "race." is a historical imposition given content and form through the proliferation of ideas imposed and claimed through law. This is not to say that people labeled "white" are not real. Rather, I mean to convey that "white" as a category of human organization rooted in a biological reality is anything but real. Furthermore, this is not to say that being labeled "white" has no meaning within society or an individual's experience. It has tremendous meaning. These meanings have been imposed and assigned by and through human action, rather than because the category reflects a fundamental truth of nature. If the distinction between "white" as a category of humanity produced by humans rather than nature remains unclear, this topic is central to the next two chapters that follow. In those chapters this distinction shall be drawn within a specific historical context working to ground the discussion.

One of the most confusing aspects of race is differentiating between the biological reality of race on the one hand, and the reality that the imposition of a racial group creates within society on the other. In other words, one's racial classification can have tremendous *social* meaning attached to it, resulting in very real and concrete consequences, even while the category itself represents no necessary human differentiation rooted in *biology*. It is an aim of this book to help clarify this important difference.

Historiography

This exploration of the first appearance of "white" people as a group of humanity referenced in law, and the reliance upon "whites" as a significant influence in the organization of U.S. society, not only relies upon laws and policies but also draws heavily upon historical texts addressing the roots of racism. It is helpful to have a general understanding of two important areas of historical inquiry, including agreement and dispute among scholars. Scholars in the twentieth century were largely concerned with addressing whether racism produced slavery or slavery produced racism. Another area of significant debate among contemporary historians is the issue of the precise status of persons of African descent prior to the passage of laws creating permanent indenture or slavery.

Both questions are important because they factor into how we make sense of the invention of "white" people. For example, if persons of African descent were from their arrival upon British colonies made separate and distinct, understood by the masses of colonists to be inferior and relegated to the status of another's property, then the invention of the category "white" makes sense largely as a rhetorical convenience, a shorthand for referencing a growing variety of peoples who joined the British in the colony. Some people were already grouped and named by the British (e.g., Indians, Negroes) but the remainder were referenced by their nationality (e.g., Dutch, Portuguese) while enactments sought to lump them together as "English and other Christians" or "English and other freeborns." On the other hand, if the status of Africans prior to the institutionalization of slavery overlapped more significantly with that of British servants, then the invention of "whites" may make more sense as a tool to facilitate a restructuring of colonial society.

There is tremendous confusion about the status of Africans prior to the institutionalization of slavery, in part because the term "slave" was rarely applied to Africans prior to the 1640s and because European servants were sometimes called slaves. According to Audrey Smedley, the reference to European servants as slaves was most likely an expression of "the subjective feelings of those who held positions as owners and masters" (2007: 99). Some historians claim that the status of Africans can be found within the existing roles of British servants. These roles included tenant, bond servant, and apprentice. Each role was for a term of years ranging from four to fourteen. Historians Oscar and Mary Handlin concluded that the first African people brought into the British colony at Jamestown in 1619 among the "cargo" of people sold from a Dutch trading ship were not slaves (1950). It is worth noting that European servants were regularly purchased from ship captains. Yet other historians of the colonial period claim that the status of Africans is entirely unclear, and surmise that it is most likely that they arrived as slaves (Morgan 1975: 154). At this point, I simply want to raise the topic as one of tremendous importance and serious dispute. The question will be pursued in more detail in the next chapter.

Whether racism preceded slavery is another question for which historians dispute the answer. Winthrop Jordan, in the important historical text *White Over Black*, argues that the English came to the colonies with racial animus toward Africans firmly entrenched (1968). Jordan viewed English hostility toward Africans as the result of negative meanings associated with blackness. In English language and culture, the color black includes such negative meanings as evil, filth, and danger, among others. Such a negative conceptualization of blackness, Jordan argues, may have paved the way for hostility from the British toward persons of African descent (1968: 7-8). Historian Carl Degler agrees with Jordan that English language and culture predisposed the British to a negative perception of Africans (1959-1960).

This argument has been firmly contested by a number of historians who have shown that, prior to the 1680s, there is significant evidence to suggest that those who would become "white" (English and certain other Europeans) were treated in a similar fashion to Africans within colonial North America and engaged in daily life on equal footing (E. Morgan 1975; P. Morgan 1998; Parent 2003; Rowe 1989). "In certain places and at certain times between 1607 and 1800, the 'lower sorts' of whites appear to have been pleasantly lacking in racial consciousness" according to David R. Roediger (1991). There is a significant historical record revealing that both African and European men "serving the same master worked, ate, and slept together, and together shared in escapades, escapes, and punishments" (Morgan 1975: 155). Some ethnographic evidence supporting this position will be explored in the following chapter.

There is also evidence that being born free was the critical measure of access to rights and privileges in law and, therefore, persons of African descent who held this status had access to all such rights, including the right to vote. In fact, there is evidence that free Africans held bond laborers (Jordan 1968: 74-75). Historian Edmund Morgan states that colonists in Virginia during the 1660s and 1670s were "ready to think of Negroes as members or potential members of the community on the same terms as other men and to demand of them the same standards of behavior" (1975: 155). Furthermore, it is noteworthy that marriage among those of African descent, mostly men, and those of European descent, mostly women, were not unusual and appear to have been met with acceptance (Smedley 2007: 105).

The body of historical evidence suggests that slavery did not emerge as a result of widespread British animosity and hostility toward Africans because of their skin color. As we will see, slavery appears to have grown out of a specific context, where both European and African laborers were treated to varying degrees as objects; the continuing demand for labor in the colonies of Virginia and Maryland was no longer being met by the shrinking pool of available men from England; a growing number of landless free Europeans were increasingly frustrated by their inability to obtain land or otherwise realize economic gain in the colony; both British and international law failed to protect Africans or any "conquered" people from slavery; and African and Europeans, laborers and free, united in opposition to the landholding elite in Bacon's Rebellion.

This brief review of two key historical inquiries, the status of Africans prior to the 1670s and whether racism preceded slavery, is by no means complete. It does, however, provide enough background from which to launch into a more detailed historical examination of these questions and consider their influence upon how we make sense of the invention of "white" people, an examination that will be pursued in the chapters that follow.

Theoretical Approach

Academic discourse on race is further complicated by terminology that asserts a "natural" status. By this, I mean that use of common race terminology such as "whites" to talk about people of European ancestry works to give a "truth" status to the social meanings that have been attached to it.

In at least two ways, use of the term "whites" plays into the belief that "whites" are a biologically occurring, distinct group of people. First, use of the term "whites" asserts the boundaries that the word "white" has been interpreted to reflect, giving credibility through the assertion itself. Second, as a category of "race," it promotes a biological meaning, because the term "race" is derived from a breeding line or stock of animals whose qualities are inheritable genetically. Anthropologist Audrey Smedley explains that "unlike other terms for classifying people (e.g., "nation," "people," "variety," "kind," and so on) the term "race" places emphasis on innateness, on the inbred nature of whatever is being judged" (2007: 40). I have found no reasonably useful way out of the conundrum that using terminology for so-called racial categories presents. As an imperfect response, I raise the concern up front and at the conclusion of the book, in an effort to fracture and destabilize the otherwise solidifying efforts of such language use.

In this book, the human category "white" is used to examine the social construction of race and the role of this human category in constituting a central theme of social organization in the United States. The book is also concerned with showing links between the invention of the human category "white" and the demise of the humanity of those so rendered.

Social constructionist theory is central to the conceptual framework for this project, directing its goals and shaping its approach to knowledge production. Social constructionism is a sociological theory of knowledge. It is a tool that helps to make sense of the body of information we hold as knowledge. Social constructionism rose to prominence in the U.S. following the publication of *The Social Construction of Reality* by Peter L. Berger and Thomas Luckmann in 1967. Berger and Luckmann argue that all knowledge, including that which is taken for granted and seen as common sense, is derived through and maintained by social interactions. Social constructionism considers how social products or phenomena are created by a particular group.

A social construct is often clarified by comparison to its opposite, essentialism. Essentialism explains and defines social products and phenomena in terms of inherent essences. Therefore, from an essentialist perspective, "white" as a category of humanity is seen as derived from nature. In other words, the category is viewed as inevitable and unrelated to human activity.

On the other hand, social constructionism explains and defines the human category "white" as a byproduct of human choices. It follows that a primary concern of social constructionism is to uncover the ways in which social products and phenomena, like the grouping "white" are created, institutionalized, known, and rendered "common sense" or "reality" by humans.

The emphasis in this book is on the construction of race and how that construction shapes "reality." Because no human is ever simply his or her race, gender, or class, these fiercely enforced social categories, among others, are approached as always intersecting and interacting. Patricia Hill Collins describes intersectionality as the examination of gender, race, class, and nation as interconnected systems that mutually construct one another (1998).[1] In other words, the construction of race often simultaneously constructs aspects of gender, class, and nationality. According to Kimberle Crenshaw, intersectionality is an approach to understanding social phenomena that factors the many statuses that constitute our political identities including: Gender, race and ethnicity, class and status in society, sexuality, physical abilities, age, national status, and so on (1991). Intersectionality helps to make visible the multiple influences that structure experiences of oppression and privilege, thereby revealing areas of divergence and commonality. Intersectional studies suggest that certain ideas and practices emerge, revealing a pattern across multiple systems of oppression, and serve as focal points for these systems (Collins 1998).

Birth of a White Nation

Both social constructionism and intersectionality become most clear in their application within a specific context. If either or both remain elusive concepts to you, just use this as an introduction to the labels. Social constructionism and intersectionality will become more concrete as they are applied to specific historical facts within a given moment in time. In chapters one and two they are central to the exploration of the invention of "white" people. The historical and legal review in chapters one and two will provide content to help these concepts become clearer.

Overview

Consistent with the goals of social constructionism and the insights of intersectional studies, this book explores how and why the human category "white" was created within the British colonies of Maryland and Virginia and became institutionalized, in part, through foundational laws within the newly formed United States of America. The meanings and working of the category "white" are explored through a variety of groups, including persons of British, African, Chinese, Japanese, Mexican, and Irish descent, among others. The experiences of these various groups in relation to the category "white" helps reveal the dynamic processes by which the category has been produced, re-produced, institutionalized and rendered common knowledge for hundreds of years.

Social constructionist theory guides what is fundamentally a project concerning epistemology, or the study of how we know what we know. In this book, law and history serve as primary sites of investigation. The particular investigation is concerned with identifying sets of taken-for-granted ways of thinking that worked to create the human category "white," and facilitated its use as a mechanism to divide laborers. There are many ways to separate people, such as religious affiliation (i.e., Jewish versus Muslim), class variations (i.e., the 1 percent who hold a majority of wealth versus the 99 percent who hold significantly less or none), ethnic height and facial features (Hutus versus Tutsis), among any number of possibilities. Why was "white" the mechanism to divide, and what is the social ethical impact of "white" as the means of doing so?

Jacqueline Battalora

Sociologist Susan Leigh Star, working within the field called the sociology of science, utilizes social constructionist theory to examine the making of scientific certainty in medicine and science. I draw upon the sociology of science and the work of Susan Leigh Star in particular to objectify constructive and persuasive efforts involved in producing, in this case, a category of humanity within a legal text (1989: 198).[2] By rendering these efforts into objects, or artifacts of knowledge production, they can be taken apart, carefully examined, and identified as one piece of a larger whole. The goal, according to Star, is to try and understand such processes over time, to try and make sense of the language and meanings held by respondents, and link them with institutional patterns and commitments. She calls on us to remember that the result (the scientific fact) could always be different.

This book argues that the group of humanity called "white" people is the product of tremendous human effort, as you will see in the chapters that follow. On the one hand, the invention affords psychological and material value to "whites," while dehumanizing and degrading on the other. The first point will be fleshed out in chapters two through four, while the latter point will be explored in the final chapter of the book.

Anti-miscegenation laws in the colony of Maryland and lawmakers' response to Bacon's Rebellion in colonial Virginia combine to help reveal the invention of the human category "white" in chapter one. "White" is revealed as one category among others competing to name the community of privilege as "British" alone became increasingly insufficient. It is shown that the human category "white" was built upon the idea of the British as white, Christian, of their essence free, and deserving of rights and privileges from which those insufficiently British-like could be denied.

Naming a group of humanity with a label that sticks is no small feat. It reflects a significant social achievement. The invention of "white" people is revealed as an extension of a compartmentalization of humanity beginning to be carved out by elite British and European colonists decades before Bacon's Rebellion, the rebellion that is held out as the critical historical event that gave rise to "white" people, and before the idea of race had any footing.

Birth of a White Nation

In chapter two, law as a labeling institution is explored. The series of laws that asserted and imposed the human category "white" and its ideological underpinnings in the decades following Bacon's Rebellion worked to discipline communities by transforming relationships among laborers and imposing a hierarchy that had not previously existed.

They also reveal ties between the invention of "whites" and a distinctly "white" patriarchal rule. British elites made connections with European laborers, in part, through the bodies of "white" women. Finally, the laws reveal the connection between the creation of a human category and the particularly exploitative version of capitalism taking hold. This version of capitalism depended upon slavery.

Immigration and naturalization law established by the First Congress of the United States reveals the success of the category "white" people. These laws worked to institutionalize whiteness as a matter of foundational law within the new republic. The ways in which whiteness shaped human relationships, labor, and the U.S. citizenry is explored in chapter three. The impact of these laws upon those viewed as "white" in the U.S., as well as those of African, Chinese, and Japanese descent, is considered.

In chapter four, the limitations of law as a labeling institution are considered through U.S. expansionism, the Treaty of Guadalupe Hidalgo, and the declaration of Mexicans as "white." The declaration of a group as "white" by federal law when there is resistance at the community level is shown as insufficient to secure the social and political benefits of whiteness. I refer to such a group as "contingent whites" because their status as "white" depends almost exclusively upon specific law, and is not generally recognized in and through everyday social interactions.[3] Mexicans were rendered not-white by state laws, with the exception of antimiscegenation law. The result is that Mexicans were rendered cheap labor, excluded from the full range of citizenship rights, and were seen as not "real" Americans.

The experience of Mexicans in relation to whiteness is contrasted with that of the Irish Catholics who were initially seen as not-white, but who succeeded in establishing their inclusion within the category. The efforts that these Irish utilized to win whiteness is revealing of the racialized political and social landscape in the U.S. and the barriers and opportunities it posed. The experience of the Irish helps shatter the commonly held belief that "white" reflects, if not genetics, then the biological state of low melanin in the skin. Large numbers of Irish Catholics arrived upon American shores with low levels of melanin. It was only by and through their ties to the Democratic Party, espousing white supremacy and their exclusion of persons of African descent from work sites, that the Irish became "white."

Chapter five reviews the patterns and commitments revealed in the histories of whiteness in the U.S. from chapters one through four, and considers why it matters in contemporary society. From its creation, whiteness has been integrally tied with the control of women and nonwhite men and the support of the wealthiest capitalists. How might a social construct with such roots, that has been imposed and enforced for more than three hundred years, be challenged? This question is pursued in chapter five. In this chapter we are reminded that revealing the human category "white" as a social construct, even one with such a lengthy history, exposes its weakness and the potential for its demise.

Let's be clear: the demise of the social construct "white" is not the same thing as the demise of the people labeled as such. Because whiteness as a facet of reality and object of knowledge is not necessary by nature, it must be constantly maintained and re-affirmed in order to persist. Challenges to the reality of "white" people and the fracturing of its knowledge-base introduce the potential for change.

This book argues that "white" is a social construct that has been assigned significant meaning. In addition, it highlights some of the ways in which this construct has shaped the humanity of "white" people and distorted the national promise of liberty, freedom and equal opportunity for all who will work hard. The Afterward considers how whiteness has impacted white people's humanity and explores why those who benefit from the social construction of whiteness would work to dismantle it.

CHAPTER 1

White People: The Creation

This chapter and the next are devoted to providing an explanation for the creation of the group of humanity called "white" people. It sounds pretty outrageous to think about white people as an invention. In fact, such a claim may be perceived as offensive to some. This is so because the invention has been such a success. In fact, many people today understand themselves to be racially white and view race as a biological fact. Such a perspective is completely understandable when forms utilized by the U.S. government, medical providers, and schools ask for a racial designation. Such common social practices make both "race" and the groups listed under it seem real. In fact, they work to make these groups "real" in the sense that they give groups meaning in society and work to make them different.

In spite of this common experience of "race," we should begin by realizing that "white" people as a designation of a group of humanity, much less as a race, never existed until late in the seventeenth century. This means that "white" people have been in existence for a very short period of time, while people whose skin reflects light skin pigmentation have been in existence for thousands of years.[4] Long before the colonists arrived upon the shores of North America, people referred to a person as a color in relation to the appearance of her or his skin as in William Shakespeare's *Othello* (1604). However, these descriptions were just that—descriptive, much like a person can be said to have yellow or brown hair. Descriptive terminology creates a visual context. Such descriptions generally do not presuppose a human difference that is thought to constitute a distinct human order or unique race.

Prior to the label "white," people were referenced by a number of possibilities, including national origin (such as Spanish, British, or Brazilian), or by religion (such as Jew, Christian, or Muslim). There were other possibilities as well, such as one's status as servant or free, owning class or servant class. However, "whites" or "white" people was not one of them. It should also be noted that "white" designating a group conceived of as united by *race* was an invention upon the invention. In other words, at the time "white" people were invented, they were not seen as a race. This occurred later and will be discussed in the next chapter.

The label "white" reflecting a group of humanity appears nowhere in law until 1681. It first appears in an enactment passed by the Colonial Assembly of the Colony of Maryland. The question is why? Who were "white" people prior to the invention? What did it mean when they became "white"? What was the problem that lawmakers sought to address through the imposition of this new category of humanity?

This chapter will explore the initial appearance of this group of humanity called "whites," addressing the motivations for the creation, those who constituted this group, and ideas that helped give rise to the new category of humanity. We will look into why "white" was selected over other possibilities. Finally, we will examine constructive (i.e., pieces that combined to create the category) and persuasive (i.e., efforts to make the category make sense) efforts deployed in the creation of "whites." These constructive and persuasive efforts will help us to identify institutional commitments. Chapter two will explore the legal and social effort involved in making the label stick. In that chapter we will consider how the label was imposed, how it functioned to alter colonial society, and how and when it began to be conceptualized as a race.

The exploration of the human group called "white" within law is instructive, even if not all-inclusive, because law is the principal means by which a society defines and regulates itself (Kelman, 1987). Significantly, law is a legitimizing institution giving preference to one version of events over others, to one description among many, to a specific policy or practice among others. Law does not produce meaning, give authority, or establish boundaries in a vacuum but rather within a larger social context, in dynamic interaction with prevailing social forces and pressures. Because of these functions, law is an important arena through which to explore and understand social phenomena. This chapter relies heavily upon colonial North American enactments and the historical record of life among laborers both preceding and following a significant expression of discontent called Bacon's Rebellion that will be discussed later in the chapter. Bacon's Rebellion represents a critical historical moment that gave rise to fear among the elite. That fear was ultimately alleviated through the invention of "white" people.

Because few people study social relations in early colonial North American history beyond the Thanksgiving story, I have taken the liberty of painting a picture with a broad stroke. Most students are familiar with post-slavery relations between "whites" and persons of African descent. In fact, this understanding is so well entrenched that many have difficulty imagining anything else. For most, it is surprising to learn that from 1619 through the 1680s in Virginia, and up to 1800 in other areas, interactions suggesting significant trust and mutuality between Europeans and Africans were not uncommon. There is rich documentation of friendly, co-conspiratorial, and loving relations between those of European and African ancestry some of which will be explored below.

Students struggle to grasp the time period in Colonial North America before slavery became entrenched. This is so, in part, because there is little understanding of the condition of poor British and Europeans who constituted the vast majority of the population, and because there is a strong tendency to interpret the past through powerful ideological frameworks within the present.

In an effort to help capture this moment in early colonial North American history, I will focus on the colony of Virginia. Virginia is significant because it was central to the invention of "white" people. It was an early colony with English settlers arriving first in 1585, then again in 1607, while the colony of Maryland was not planted until 1633. Virginia was the site of Bacon's Rebellion in the 1670s, which was followed by dramatic changes in law that created a new (much lower) bottom to the social hierarchy and assigned this location to those of African descent.

Colonial Virginia Before the Institution of Black Slavery

The Virginia colony was pursued in 1585 with lofty goals. Englishmen Walter Raleigh and Richard Hakluyt convinced Queen Elizabeth to support the establishment of the colony to serve as a hub for attacks on Spanish settlements, and advance the riches of the Crown while decreasing those of Spain (Morgan 1975: 25-28). The colony was to serve as an employer for England's growing numbers of unemployed and create new markets for her goods among the native tribes and settlers, as well as bring the natives into the fold of Christianity and the British government. By 1590 the settlement was found deserted, without a record of what happened to the English settlers (Ibid. at 42).

The next effort to colonize Virginia began with 105 settlers in 1607 as a corporate endeavor intended to increase the investments of shareholders of The Virginia Company of London.[5] The governor of the colony recruited vigorously. By 1624 over four thousand British settlers had come to the colony, but less than a thousand survived.[6] In 1619, just over twenty people from Africa were recorded in the colony. It is unclear how many survived by 1624. The death rate was shocking, and the king dissolved the company and placed it under control of the crown. The demand for laborers continued despite the low survival rate, in part because tobacco was being grown and shipped to England. Tobacco farming required significant human labor and so helped fuel the demand for farm workers. Tobacco held the hope of riches for many.

Between 1607 and 1682 roughly 92,000 immigrants from Europe were brought, mostly to the Virginia colony but also to Maryland, and more than three-quarters of these immigrants – or more than 69,000 – were chattel bond laborers (Allen 1997: 119).[7] Most were men, and most were English. In Virginia until approximately 1640, there were seven males twenty years of age or older for every woman (Wells 1975: 164). The sex ratio improved significantly by 1700, but remained high because of the large numbers of indentured servants from Europe imported into the colony, most of whom were males. The sex ratio in Virginia is thought to be similar to that of Maryland, where few women were among the first colonists and a sex imbalance remained until the Civil War (Ibid.).

Getting to the colony was one thing; surviving there was another. The colony grew from about 1,300 settlers in 1625 to about 2,600 by 1629, 8,000 by 1640, more than 14,000 by 1653, and 25,000 by 1660 (Morgan 1975: 136). It is estimated that there were only about five hundred persons of African descent in the Virginia colony by 1650. There was also a substantial minority of others who were not English, including Portuguese, Spanish, French, Turk and Dutch. The growing population reflects not an increase in the flow of immigrants to the colony, but an advancing survival rate. By raising cattle and other grazing animals in addition to farming corn and planting orchards, Virginians were able to feed themselves and improve their health.

English laborers came to the colony in one of several statuses: tenant, bond servant, or apprentice. Tenants were under the supervision of a company agent and entitled to one-half of the returns earned. Bond servants belonged to their master. The master supplied the servant with food, clothing, and shelter during the years of service, and the master got everything earned by the servant. Apprentices were bound as servants for seven years and then another seven years as a tenant to the planter, who paid ten pounds for the laborer. Historian Edmund S. Morgan notes that it is likely that the majority of the men were sent as tenants, but that abuses of laborers and the addition of terms of years by masters were not uncommon (1975: 116-121, 126-128). In fact, the treatment of servants in Virginia by their masters shocked other Englishmen. Large numbers of Europeans were regularly bought and sold "like horses" in Virginia. Most Europeans came to Virginia with only varying degrees or future promises of freedom. To put it another way, most people arrived in Virginia being unfree to some degree.

While large numbers of laborers were working to their death in Virginia, some officers in the colony were getting rich. The beginnings of this colony reveal a private enterprise operating with few checks and balances, advancing the fortunes of a few and the death of many. It is important to remember that at this time, the vast majority of laborers in Virginia were Englishmen. Morgan remarks on this period of the Virginia colony, stating that a "servant, by going to Virginia, became for a number of years a thing, a commodity with a price," and he concludes that we "may also see Virginians beginning to move toward a system of labor that treated men as things" (1975: 129). According to Theodore Allen, landowners accumulating wealth from tobacco in 1620s Virginia transformed European tenants and wage laborers into "chattel bond-servitude" (1997: 178). European servitude in the tobacco fields of Virginia, claims Morgan, came closer to slavery than anything the British had ever seen (1975: 296).

The status of the first African colonists in Virginia is indeterminate. What is certain is that within the decades before 1680, some Africans were free or became so. Africans worked for masters alongside British laborers. There is plenty of ethnographic material revealing that at least some persons of African descent were not treated as degraded beings, and behaved in manners consistent with Englishmen of a similar class. That persons of African descent were treated in a disparate manner by some Europeans at some moments in time cannot be disputed, and evidence of such will be discussed later in the chapter. However, the entire body of available documents weighs much heavier with evidence of Europeans and Africans interacting in ways that suggest cooperation and a degree of mutuality.

Records that help to paint a picture of the status of Africans prior to 1680 are scarce. Those that have been retrieved reveal that antipathy directed at persons of African descent did not define the social landscape. If, as some historians have argued, English people had a "natural" antipathy toward persons with dark skin, you would not expect British or other Europeans to treat persons of African descent as equals, or as desirable other than as labor.[8] Furthermore, if persons of African descent were accustomed to being treated in a degrading manner by Europeans, then you would expect a fearful and possibly subservient posture as a result of accumulated insult and injury. Neither is the case with any consistency.

Instead, the evidence shows that many African men married European servants, and these marriages appear to have been accepted. Because there were five to seven times more men than women in the colony, a woman could likely have her pick. In one case, an African servant sued successfully for her freedom and married the European lawyer who represented her in court (Allen 1997: 195-6). If such a marriage were viewed by local Virginians as an affront to the British then you would expect to find the lawyer shunned or otherwise harmed, but the marriage did not seem to diminish the lawyer's social position.

Historian Philip Morgan provides detailed descriptions of relationships between persons of European and African descent during the colonial period in North America (1998). For example, the European widow of an African planter next married a European farmer without issue. Again, if there was stigmatization attached to a European woman having married an African man, then we would expect the widow to be rejected by European men as a potential spouse. This does not appear to be the case. Another piece of ethnographic material reveals that a European female servant told her European master that she would rather marry an African slave on a nearby plantation than marry him, despite his wealth. That is exactly what she did (Morgan 1998).

Women outlived men and widows regularly remarried, bringing land and animals to their marriages. Records from one county show that in the 1660s, one-fourth of all children born to European female servants were of joint African and European ancestry. Records from an Eastern Shore colonial county reveal that five of the ten free African men there were married to European women (Parent 2003).

Resistance to governmental authority was common among the British and shared by at least some men of African descent. For example, a particularly descriptive court deposition describes an African property owner who was approached by a European messenger of the court delivering a subpoena. The owner responded with contempt. The messenger informed him that he should appear to testify, but instead the landowner flogged him and sent the messenger away, stating that he would appear when he pleased, after his corn was harvested (Morgan 1975: 156-7).

Edmund Morgan references numerous wills wherein masters set up conditions "whereby Negro slaves would become free or could purchase their freedom. And the terms indicate an expectation that they would become regular members of the free community" (1975: 156). Furthermore, both European and African men working for the same master slept, ate, and labored together. Court records of this period reveal that Europeans and Africans joined together in escapes and criminal endeavors. Such joint ventures suggest trust and cooperation, qualities of a relationship that stand in opposition to animosity on the basis of color. There is ample evidence from court records that Europeans and Africans of the same class behaved similarly and were treated so by courts.

Until 1662, both persons of African and European ancestry appear to have been treated similarly for sexual violations.[9] Each stood in church with the customary white sheet and white wand to do penance for fornication or for having committed adultery (Morgan 1975: 155-56). There is still more evidence of trust and cooperation between Europeans and Africans. G.S. Rowe's study of defendants of African descent in the criminal courts of Philadelphia in the late eighteenth century reveal that both Europeans and Africans of the lower classes accepted each other, as evidenced by shared ventures that required trust and cooperation (1989: 695). This was not the case, however, among the more economically privileged Europeans. The overwhelming evidence suggests that, prior to the 1680s in Virginia, Maryland and Carolina, and as late as 1800 in areas of New England, European antipathy toward persons of African descent because of their skin color was not widespread.

As we prepare to explore the first appearance of "white" reflecting a distinct group of humanity in law, a general overview of the legal landscape out of which it emerged is instructive. It is not possible in the space of this chapter to articulate, even briefly, the full legal context of the Colonial Era along the eastern seaboard of what became the U.S. Therefore, those areas of society and law that the law under consideration most interacted with and depended upon will be explored. They include the social and legal significance of marriage, the law regulating the status of a child, and other laws and social practices that laid the groundwork for human division.

Colonial North America: A Social and Legal Context

The colonial Assemblies of Maryland and Virginia stood at the forefront of the development of laws that promulgated and imposed the human category "white." Colonial enactments from these colonies are central to an exploration of the invention of "white" people. Both colonies shared an economy heavily invested in the farming of tobacco, a crop demanding tremendous human labor.

Colonists brought with them the patriarchal order of the household that existed in pre-modern England. The context within which each colony engaged in the work of establishing the parameters of community, as a matter of definition and regulation, was guided by British common law. It provided the basis for the system of law, including marriage. Common law provided a clear directive regarding women's place in marriage as captured by Sir William Blackstone:

> By marriage, the husband and wife are one person in law: that is, the very being or legal existence of the woman is suspended during marriage, or at least is incorporated and consolidates into that of the husband; under whose wing, protection, and cover, she performs everything (Salmon 1979: 94).

In other words, the traditional common law conception of marital unity was that "man and wife are one – but the man is the one" (Williams 1947: 18). The male head of the household was assumed to represent the interests of a family. Under common law, marriage placed firmly within the control of a husband all property ownership, all economic matters concerning the household, the custody of children, and the responsibility to govern a wife's behavior. He was expected to provide materially and to protect all women, children, and other dependents within the household, in exchange for the obedience of women and children.[10]

This model of marriage was carried into the colonies and eventually incorporated within U.S. law (Blood and Wolf 1960). Indeed, well into the nineteenth century, a married woman in the U.S. was unable to hold title to property in her own name, including property inherited or which was bequeathed to her, retain her own wages, enter into contracts, or to acquire custody of her children in the case of legal separation (Basch 1984: 42-69).

North American colonial law largely replicated the common law of Great Britain, as in the case of marriage noted above. However, not every law in the colonies was consistent with British common law. Colonial enactments that are inconsistent reveal a great deal about the specific context the colonists faced and the constraints and opportunities it posed for those in positions of power. Areas of colonial law that stand in opposition to British law include: (1) the determination of the status of a child as free or enslaved; (2) numerous areas of law concerning European laborers, including the prohibition of marriage during years of bond-servitude; and (3) marriage prohibitions, called antimiscegenation laws, that punished an English person who married a specifically identified "other." Each reflects a dramatic break from British law. British common law was being deftly altered to take advantage of the new economic opportunities offered by unique colonial social conditions. This is revealing not only of the particular forces and pressures and opportunities that the colonial context presented, but also of the role of law as a means to address them.

The rule of law in England, *partus sequitir patrem*, made the status of the child dependent upon the condition of the father. In 1662 the General Assembly of the Virginia Colony made a "mulatto" child's status as free or slave dependent upon the condition of the child's mother, marking a dramatic shift from British law (Hening 2:170).

As African laborers began to be synonymous with life-service or slavery at the end of the seventeenth century, the law worked to render the children of women of African descent human capital. Black women were transformed into a machinery of capitalist production. The law permitted and encouraged the sexual violation of black women as a means of increasing plantation wealth.

This law dramatically impacted British (eventually white) women as well. They became the only possible production site of "pure" British (eventually white) children. Steve Martinot explains:

> Sexuality was devalued in English women in the process of relocating it in the bodies of African Women. That is, by validating the violation of African women as the cultural site of sexuality itself, in the name of and in the interest of plantation wealth, sexual being was in the same gesture withheld from English women. English women became instead the desexualized site of validated motherhood as the concomitant of the commodification of African motherhood

as capital. Motherhood was functionalized for English women in the process of appropriating motherhood as production in the African (2010: 40-41).

Through this law, black women's reproduction advanced the property value of the plantation while English women's reproduction ensured "pure" inheritors of this property. Virginia's formula for determining the status of a mulatto child was adopted by every southern commonwealth with the exception of Maryland.[11] This law's existence and wide acceptance reflects its ability to serve the interests of the most powerful colonists, specifically those most invested in unpaid and underpaid labor.

In the colonies, marriage was prohibited during years of bond-servitude unless the master consented. This was not the case in England, where the marriage of servants was viewed as necessary for the production of the next generation of servant class laborers. This was not the only difference. Servants in the colony faced longer terms and much more severe treatment than their counterparts in England. In the colonies, exclusion from marriage combined with laws that punished premarital and extra-marital sex and extended years of service when a child was born outside of marriage, to render women in bond-servitude particularly vulnerable to sexual exploitation and to the extended exploitation of their labor (Hening 1643, 1: 252-253; *Arch. Md.* 1640, 1:97; Hening 3: 74, 139, 361).

These laws combined to create particularly harsh conditions for women laborers and reveal something of the type of capitalism taking hold. In this version of capitalism, conditions were being structured to set female reproduction against labor. The laws stretched the years of servitude owed beyond the original agreement and without compensation. Through such enactments, labor was rendered less hospitable to women than men, while the value of family (at least among the masses of people in the colony) was devalued. The degree of labor exploitation upon which the version of capitalism taking hold depended will prove to be a pattern in the colony and later in the U.S.

Another area of law that diverges from British common law is that of antimiscegenation. Because this area of law is the site of the first appearance of "white" people, it will be explained and addressed in its own section that follows.

Antimiscegenation Law

Antimiscegenation law, advancing what would become "racial" restrictions on marriage, saw the invention of the category "white," reflecting a distinct group of people. These laws prohibited a "white" person from marrying specific categories of persons seen as not "white." Such "mixing" would eventually be called "miscegenation,"[12] and the laws that prohibited such relations would be referred to as "antimiscegenation" laws (Getman 1984:122-23). The crime of miscegenation was shaped and reshaped over time in response to and as a reflection of political, economic, ethical and psychological needs and desires of the British ruling elite as they interacted with and responded to the free Europeans of the colonies. The creation of this new body of crime, called *miscegenation*, created a criminal that did not steal goods or inflict physical violence.

No law stands alone. Legislation comes about largely because lawmakers perceive a deficiency in existing laws as they interact with cultural practices and/or social change. It does not make much sense for lawmakers to go through the trouble of crafting and then passing legislation unless it addresses a need or desire. What was the need addressed or desire served by the first law in which "white" referencing a group of humanity appears? In order to explore this question we first must understand some things about this body of law.

Antimiscegenation law references those laws that imposed restrictions upon marriage that prohibited a member of a group understood by lawmakers to be superior from marrying a person of the opposite sex who was a member of a group they believed to be inferior.[13] These laws, for example, prohibited a "white" person from marrying a person of African descent. Like the human category "white," antimiscegenation law was an invention of North American colonists and reflects a dynamic interaction of gender relations, social control measures, and economic and power-gaining opportunities within the colonial context.

This arena of law provides an important entranceway into the invention and evolving understanding of the category "white" and the role of law in the inventive enterprise. Why? Because examining antimiscegenation law provides a number of insights. First, it helps inform the parameters that influenced those thought to be "white." Second, it reveals meanings that were predicated to this new group of humanity. Third, because antimiscegenation law pre-existed the first use of the human category "white" in law and because antimiscegenation law served as a site of significance to the new category, this area of law is insightful to the inventive effort itself, helping to answer the "why white?" question.

Antimiscegenation law was neither derived from the statutory laws of antiquity nor from the common law of England, but was a creation of colonial North America. It was in an environment wherein marriageable women were in short supply and the location of power within marriage was held almost exclusively by the husband that the first antimiscegenation law was enacted. In this statute, a British woman and an African man were being portrayed as members of sufficiently different human groups to require the enactment of a marriage prohibition.

The Colonial Assembly of Maryland in 1664 enacted a law that punished a woman who was "English or freeborn" who married a black slave (*Arch. Md.* 1: 526-527). The law stated in part:

> ...for preuention whereof for deterring such (English and) free borne women from such shamefull Matches . . .whatsoeuer free borne woman shall inter marry with any slaue . . . shall Serue the master of such slaue during the life of her husband And that all the Issue of such free borne women soe marryed shall be Slaues as their fathers were (Ibid. at 527).

While Maryland law did not void the marriage, it did legislate harsh consequences for the woman who entered into it and to any children of the couple. She faced life service to the master of her husband for the duration of her husband's life, while any children of the couple were rendered slaves. In these ways, the law worked as a deterrent to these marriages, the express intent of the law. However, prevention and deterrence were not the only forces at work.

For slaveholders, there was incentive to encourage English or other freeborn women to enter into marriages with enslaved African men. The law worked to enlarge their slaveholdings by adding not only the new bride, but also any children the couple might have. As a result, there was encouragement for slaveholders to promote these marriages. In 1681 the Maryland Assembly corrected for the conflicting messages within the Maryland Enactment of 1664. The 1681 enactment will be discussed later in the chapter.

The three areas of colonial law discussed above that stand in opposition to British law are highlighted here because they provide important legal context for the emergence of "white" people. The invention of "white" people in law represents a moment in time when a line is drawn in the sand. It represents a linguistic divide separating those who are within it from those excluded from it. While "negro" and "Indian" already served to separate and divide, "white" sharpened those divisions by erasing divisions within and among British and Europeans of the colonies. At the same time, it represents a need or desire and reveals a commitment in the colonies to a particular version of capitalism that stands in opposition to a shared sense of humanity and in opposition to "the family" in favor of human hierarchies and cruel extensions of labor. These colonial laws also lay the foundation for a division of humanity that will be accelerated by the invention of "white" people.

The laws are important, in part, because they are contrary to British common law, and therefore suggest needs and desires particular to the colonial North American context. But the question remains: whose needs and desires? A law may reflect the sentiment of some, most, or few of the people in the community. It is fairly obvious that the law rendering the status of a child dependent upon the status of the mother, and the law that imposed additional years of service for a child born during one's years of bond-servitude, served the interests of those invested in plantation labor and worked against the interests of the masses of laborers. What is often missed is that these extensions of labor also harmed European and African farmers who were free of servitude, because it is hard to compete with the farmer who has free labor. Large landholders who extended years of servitude among servants without pay could produce more for less.

What about the law that punished a British or freeborn woman who married a slave of African descent? Does this law reflect a widely held belief that people were in need of separation, specifically English women from black men? There is a wealth of information, some of which has been previously noted, that suggests that the lawmakers' sentiments regarding the impropriety of "English" and other "free born" women marrying black slaves was not shared by the masses within the colonies.

Creating Difference In Law

The degree of similarity of treatment between those of African descent and those who would become "white," prior to 1680 in Virginia and Maryland and up to 1800 in other areas, is well established (E. Morgan 1975; Parent 2003; P. Morgan 1998; Rowe 1989). There is also evidence of different treatment. It is in those areas where treatment was not similar that clues might be found to help explain the emergence of the human category "white." Evidence of different treatment is not reviewed here because it overshadows the evidence that Europeans and Africans engaged in relationships of trust and mutuality. It does not. Rather, it is important in order to make visible the process that eventually gave rise to the social and legal change in the colony that dramatically altered those relationships of mutuality, cooperation and trust between persons of African and European ancestry.

For example, the experience of coming to the colonies was different. European bond laborers entered contracts for their labor and traveled, without literal chains, across the Atlantic. The journey took between eight to twelve weeks and was difficult. Indentured servants were packed into the hull of the ship with little or no fresh air and were given a ration of bread every two weeks. In contrast, African laborers were exclusively stolen people forced through the middle passage in chains under grueling conditions.[14] Winthrop Jordan highlights another way in which Africans were set apart from British and Europeans generally – the label "negroes" (1968: 73). Similarly, native tribal members were set apart from the English not only by the word "Indians" but by their treatment (Lauber 1913).

Another example of differential treatment can be seen when, in 1640, the Virginia General Court pronounced the sentence for three servants who temporarily escaped. The Dutchman and the Scot were ordered four additional years of service while the third servant, "a negro

.... shall serve his master or his assigns for the time of his natural life ..." (Jordan 1968: 75).[15] Add to this the Maryland antimiscegenation law of 1664 and the Virginia fornication law of 1662, wherein lawmakers doubled the fine imposed for sexual intimacy outside of marriage when one party was "English or Christian" and the other party was "negro," and there is some evidence that *among lawmakers,* distinctions between Europeans and Africans were being crafted and expressed through law (*Arch. Md.* 1: 526-527; Hening 2: 170). There are all kinds of distinctions among and between people reflected in law, such as plaintiff and defendant, lessor and lessee, victim and accused, and buyer and seller, to mention just a few. What makes the distinctions noted in the laws above so noteworthy is that they are distinctions that the invention of "white" people presumed and worked to accelerate and sharpen.

The Maryland and Virginia laws noted above reveal that during the 1660s, within the arena of sexuality and marriage, persons of African descent and members of native tribes were being constructed by lawmakers, though not by the masses of laborers, as sufficiently unlike the British so as to justify what was at that point an ethnic-based marriage prohibition and different, more harsh treatment in law.[16] Similarly, the dramatic sex imbalance that existed in Maryland could very well have been a motivating force for the antimiscegenation law in that colony, rather than animus toward black Africans. However, legal descriptions within the enactment of 1664 suggest the emergence of an understanding of human difference between those viewed as like the British on the one hand, who were seen as superior, and on the other hand, those viewed as clearly not like the British, who were seen as inferior. What is certain is that these laws reveal that those of African descent and members of native tribes *began* to be reflected in law as different from those who were seen as sufficiently like the English as early as the 1660s (Hening 2:170; *Arch. Md.* 1:526-527).

The evidence of different treatment noted above should not be construed as a challenge to the interpretations of historians who claim that prior to the 1680s, there is "little clear evidence of uniform or widespread social antipathy on account of their [blacks'] color." (Smedley 2007: 104-105). It does suggest that historian Edmund Morgan's claim, that Virginia colonists of the 1660s and 1670s were poised to think of Africans as potential members of the community on the same terms as other men (1975: 155), requires some modification, as this sentiment is not clearly reflected by Virginia's lawmakers at this time even if it was supported by the actions of laborers. What the Maryland antimiscegenation law of 1664 and the Virginia fornication law of 1662 present is a record, prior to the 1680s, that shows those who will become "white" (i.e., those seen as like the English) being constructed in law as sufficiently different from those of African descent and members of native tribes, by those exerting legal authority within these colonies (*Arch. Md.* 1: 526-527; Hening 2: 170).

In Virginia, a law was enacted in 1640 that prohibited those of African descent from possessing firearms; however, the law appears to have been ignored and unenforced (Breede and Innis 1980). This 1640 enactment is noteworthy because it suggests a very early sign of a desire on the part of lawmakers to treat Africans in an inferior manner. It is equally noteworthy that this effort was apparently rejected by the community.

These laws build upon the law that linked the status of a child with that of her mother, and set the groundwork for the invention of "whites" by starting to divide people in ways that the invention of "white" people dramatically accelerated. They reveal an understanding of perceived human difference rooted in sufficient likeness or unlikeness to the British. Finally, they help to reveal institutional patterns and commitments that will be elaborated upon later.

Bacon's Rebellion

Bacon's Rebellion occurred at a time when the survival rate had significantly improved and the numbers of tenants and servants who completed their terms (not to mention survived) was growing. While survival and completion of terms of indenture were positive outcomes for laborers, they posed problems for those who governed. These changes meant more competition for large landholders as freed tenants sought their own fortunes in tobacco, adding to the supply and depressing the price.

These free men, most of whom were bachelors, presented a growing threat to British authorities in Virginia. They responded to this threat by extending years of servitude and increasing the term of service required as a penalty for such violations as running away, giving birth to a child, or killing a hog. In 1670 a law was enacted that stripped these men of their ability to vote so that only landowners and keepers of homes could vote in elections (Hening 2: 280).

As the numbers of freed tenants and servants grew in the 1640s and 1650s, fewer and fewer could expect to hold public office or to find workable land that was not already claimed. Indentured servants faced harsher conditions, while freed ones faced narrowing opportunities for financial independence. Falling tobacco prices, combined with taxation from the crown and the relative exclusion of most colonists from participating in the fur trade, all worked to increase the resentment of the indentured and freed.

Other conditions had changed as well. Recalling that Virginia's economy was deeply invested in tobacco and that the farming of tobacco required tremendous human effort, the desire for laborers failed to decline. Recalling also that the vast majority of laborers who arrived in Virginia every year were Englishmen, changes in this labor supply would have a noticeable impact upon the colony. By mid-century the poor and homeless who were sent from England slowed significantly, leaving a gap in the labor supply. British landholders in Virginia had to look elsewhere, and in the decades that followed the numbers of laborers from Africa began to increase significantly.

The numbers of discontented Virginians were many. Servants of African and European descent faced harsher treatment while those freed from servitude confronted conditions that rendered their freedom from servitude, much less their success, more and more tenuous.

In 1676, these discontented people erupted in the colony of Virginia with laborers of European and African descent, bond and free, uniting in the fight against unpaid labor, the plantation elite, and those governing the colony, in an effort to realize greater opportunity and independence. Bacon's Rebellion was complicated and nuanced. Here, I will provide only a brief overview. There was a first phase that focused upon attacking native tribes, and a second phase that was a direct challenge to the British who ruled the colony. The rebels expressed disdain for the way they ruled and grew their wealth.

Birth of a White Nation

The rebellion is named after the man who led it, Nathaniel Bacon. He and a number of his neighbors held contempt for native tribal members, who they blamed for the death of numerous servants. These neighbors were unimpressed by the response of the government to these incidents, and were increasingly perturbed by the cost of the government that they supported through taxes. Bacon himself was a member of the governing council and tried without success to get a commission from Governor Berkley to attack native tribes. Bacon proceeded without it and on May 10, 1676, the governor denounced Bacon and removed him from the council. Bacon proceeded to lead a crusade against all native tribes, friendly and hostile, those with whom the Virginia colony had agreements and those with whom it did not.

Bacon was decreed a rebel by Governor Berkley while Bacon issued a "Declaration of the People" that sought to ruin all native tribes, including all trade with them. In addition, he began advocating for a redistribution of some of the ill-gotten wealth in the colony. According to Morgan, "[i]n a society where success had always depended on exploitation that fell short of plunder, it was an appealing formula to men of every class" (1975: 255). Within an environment of tremendous discontent among poorly treated laborers from Africa and Europe and more constraints with fewer opportunities for the growing numbers of freed servants, it was not hard to rally supporters for Bacon's cause. While Bacon continued to attack native tribes, other rebel groups plundered the estates of government loyalists. In late October, Bacon died. Soon thereafter, armed ships from England arrived and the rebellious tide died out, but not without having made an impact. Bacon's Rebellion represents the unification of laborers of African and European descent, freed servants, and small landowners. The threat of a united labor force to the capitalist plantation system was clear. The response by the governing elite was a divide and conquer approach. They separated laborers by creating one group with the authority to rule over and oppress the other.

Historian Gary Nash, in describing the process of imposing slavery upon persons of African descent, provides a succinct review of the legal response that followed Bacon's Rebellion:

> In rapid succession Afro-Americans lost their right to testify before a court, to engage in any kind of commercial activity, either as buyer or seller; to hold property; to participate in the political process; to congregate in public places with more than two or three of their fellows; to travel without permission; and to engage in legal marriage or parenthood (1992: 159).

According to Theodore W. Allen, the response to the rebellion was the creation of a new social status that would be a birthright of Anglos as well as Europeans in North America, a "white" identity designed to set them apart from African bond laborers as well as enlist Europeans across class lines as active or passive supporters of capitalist agriculture based on chattel bond labor (1997: 167).

Bacon's Rebellion provides the rationale to explain the need to divide laborers as a means of social control. A more detailed look at the response of colonial legislators to Bacon's Rebellion reveals such an undertaking in law, and will be examined in the next chapter. However, neither the rebellion nor the response to it explains why "white" was procured as the means to do so. There is always more than one way to accomplish a task - here, the division of laborers.

Why "White"?

In the aftermath of Bacon's Rebellion, Virginia's landowning elite pushed for legislation that set "British and other whites" apart from those of native tribes, mulattos, and those of African descent. These laws emerged in Virginia from 1691 through the first quarter of the eighteenth century. The inclusion of antimiscegenation law among the list of benefits and privileges afforded to "whites" by law suggests that the law was less of a control mechanism to restrict "whites" than a benefit to advance interests. This claim will be advanced in the next chapter.

It was not within an enactment from the Virginia colony where Bacon's Rebellion raged that "white" referencing a group of humanity first appears, but rather, in an enactment from the colony of Maryland. Recalling that Maryland's antimiscegenation law of 1664 had the effect of encouraging the very marriages the law explicitly claimed to prevent, Maryland legislators sought to address the conflict in 1681.

The law included financial disincentives to masters who encouraged or assisted such marriages and imposed fines upon the priest, minister, or magistrate who performed the marriage (*Arch. Md.* 7: 204). The law states in part:

> And for as much diverse freeborn English or White woman sometimes by the Instigacon Procurement or Convenience of theire Masters Mistres or dames....doe intermarry with Negroes & Slaves....." (Ibid.).

The switch from the use of "English or freeborn" as the critical category referenced in the 1664 legislation requiring protection to that of "white" women can be seen in this law.

Virginia enacted an antimiscegenation law in 1691 and applied its marriage prohibitions to men and women within identified groups. It punished a "white" woman or man who married a person who was of African descent or a member of a native tribe by banishing them from the colony. The law stated, in part:

> ...whatsoever English or other white man or woman being free shall intermarry with a negroe, mulatto, or Indian man or woman bond or free, shall within three months after such marriage be banished and removed from this dominion forever, ... (Hening 3: 86-88).

The 1681 antimiscegenation law of Maryland utilizes an entirely new label to reference a group of people. This new label was unlike those used in the past, which referenced nationality, religious affiliation, or legal status relative to enslavement or freedom. What explains the emergence of this new label and what is its significance? While Bacon's Rebellion explains the desire to divide laborers, why was "white" the selected mechanism to do so? Historians who have addressed the emergence of race in colonial North America fail to subject the category deployed to question. There are always multiple ways of accomplishing a task.

Maryland's antimiscegenation laws of 1664 and 1681 and Virginia's fornication law of 1662 and antimiscegenation law of 1691 reflect shifts in labels given to those who would become "white." These laws reveal that those who were members of native tribes or of African descent were viewed as sufficiently unlike the British so as to warrant separate labels and exclusion from the full package of rights and privileges that the British and those considered sufficiently like them enjoyed. This was true prior to Bacon's Rebellion, at least among lawmakers. What is striking after Bacon's Rebellion is the label given to those who were not "Negroes or mulattos or Indians." These people, who were referenced in law first primarily as "British and other Christians" and then by mid-century as "English and free born," became after 1680 "white" (*Arch. Md.* 1: 526-527; 1662, Hening 2: 170). These shifts in labels were not unique to laws restricting marriage but are apparent in the broad legal record.

The Maryland antimiscegenation law of 1681 refers to "Freeborn English and other whites" as the group of women to whom the law is directed (*Arch. Md.* 7: 204). Virginia's antimiscegenation law, enacted in 1691, references "English and other whites" as the relevant group and applies its prohibitions to both men and women (Hening 3: 86). Maryland followed suit one year later and extended its prohibition to men and women (*Arch. Md.* 1692, 13: 546-549).

What do these shifts in labels offer to an understanding of why "white" became the label to designate a group, over other possibilities? Furthermore, what do these statutes reveal about who is "white" and what "white" means in law, at least within the context of its emergence in colonial North America? Finally, and most generally, what does antimiscegenation law offer to a fuller understanding of the construction of "white" people?

The shifts in labels for those who would become "white" capture the struggle to name those who would lay claim to a "new" land. The evolution of labels within antimiscegenation law reflects a struggle to name the expanding community of privilege as the label "British" alone became increasingly insufficient, with the influx of other colonists. The first such labeling effort, "British and other Christians," was problematic because conversion to Christianity offered a relatively easy crossover. This was especially problematic with regard to those who had been identified via homogenizing labels such as "Indian" or "negro" to be unlike the British and who, beginning in the

1660s, began to be carved out in laws for separate and less favorable treatment. This anxiety is reflected in a 1664 enactment in Maryland clarifying that conversion to Christianity holds no relevance to one's status as a slave and does not lead to manumission (*Arch. Md.* 1: 526, 533; 2: 272). Freedom would not be permitted so easily.

The next labeling effort captures a status conferred at birth, thereby taking care of the conversion threat. However, the designation "English and Freeborn" presented its own limitations: the majority of tribal members were born free, while some Africans were free as well. In these ways, both "Christian" and "freeborn" were too expansive to the social order being crafted by lawmakers, capturing at least some of those who were rendered outsiders by the British elite. These attempts to name those who were English-like suggest the needed elements of a satisfactory label: one, it would require that those already identified as unlike the English be excluded, and second, it would require that the label not allow for simple conversion into the group. Bacon's Rebellion represented the unification of the masses in Virginia in opposition to native peoples, to the plantation elite as well as those who governed (these were often one on the same). As such, the rebellion provided the need for another element of a satisfactory label: it would need to facilitate the making of strong ties between large numbers of laborers and the elite of the colony. These elements helped to narrow the field of possibilities for the new label.

Previous efforts to label the community of privilege failed to develop an ideology of shared identity that was strong enough to cause laborers to see themselves as sufficiently linked to the elite British of the colony. Rather, the evidence of social relations prior to the decades following the rebellion reveal strong ties between and among laborers, whether from Africa, Ireland, England, or Portugal.

There can be little doubt that the visible differences between British and African helped facilitate the social divide created between the two, and reduction of the latter into permanent servitude. Anthropologist Audrey Smedley notes that the "visibility of Africans made it possible to structure the demarcation point of permanent slavery solely on the basis of color" (2007: 115). It is critical to an understanding of the invention of the human category "white" to recall that, while early colonists saw people who looked dramatically different from them, these differences had little *meaning* in society until the decades following Bacon's Rebellion. Post-rebellion, "the negro" was assigned new meaning as debased and servile, and was positioned below and in opposition to British and Europeans in order to accommodate the needs of the planter class. This group of British and Europeans, laborers and freemen that would stand in opposition to the African slave needed to be sufficiently aligned with the ruling British of the colonies.

It is within this context and under these constraints, desires and demands that "white" became the next label to capture the community of privilege (i.e., those sufficiently like the British) within the Virginia and Maryland colonies and all others to follow. "White" rendered inclusion within the privileged group to an element of phenotype, in other words, a physical feature that is not readily changed. As such, from the outset it could exclude the vast majority of those already clearly established by lawmakers, if not others, as insufficiently British-like. Also, unlike Christian and freeborn, "white" had no previously established firm guidelines and accepted parameters. This gave the new category incredible flexibility, and is likely a feature of its incredible survival and success. Who was "white" was by no means clearly established in 1681 and remains undefined as a matter of law to this day.

Constructive and Persuasive Efforts: Creating the Common Knowledge of Whiteness[17]

Antimiscegenation law offers insight into an understanding of what courts later term the "common knowledge" of whites. The Maryland legislators worked to shape the meaning of Britishness such that it functioned to signify freedom and the presumption of certain citizenship rights and privileges. In the eyes of the Maryland colonial lawmakers, a British woman could only enter into a marriage with an enslaved African man if she failed to acknowledge her essence: free. It is somewhat ironic that under this law, being British, as a reflection of being free, functioned as justification for a law that imposed restrictions (specifically on marital choice), although limiting the freedoms of women was nothing new.

Birth of a White Nation

The Maryland antimiscegenation law of 1664 reflects not only a constraint upon British women's interactions, but the imposition of a fragile superiority. The rights and privileges that the law recognized and protected for British and other free people, although not indefinite, could be lost by certain acts that posed a serious threat to the very meanings of British and freedom that the law both presumed and imposed.

The legislation refers to the marriage of an English woman to a slave of African descent as being to the "disgrace of our nation" (*Arch. Md.* 1: 527). This description of harm is significant for a number of reasons. It reveals that the legislators viewed the resulting harm as collectively shared. The law goes on to explain that the servitude imposed upon the woman and the children of her marriage was intended to deter British women from entering "such shameful matches" (Ibid.).

That the Maryland law imposed a marriage restriction upon English women and enslaved African men but not upon English men and enslaved women of African descent reveals, among other things, that rights and privileges were not shared equally. Important factors such as gender were significant determinants of the degree of access or restriction. The law worked to advance the privileges of English men and those viewed as sufficiently like the British, since an effect of the law was to expand the pool of available women by making them legally available *only* to them.

Within the southern colonies, the social pressure for women to marry was tremendous.[18] During this period, especially in those locations where women were scarce and in great demand, control over marriageable women is apparent.[19] The Maryland law of 1664 is one example. The law worked to direct the marital choices of English and other freeborn women.

The shift from "English and other freeborn women" to "English and other *white* women and men" as the class requiring protection is significant. The Maryland law of 1681 reflects the first time in legal history, in the land that would eventually become the U.S., that "white" was used in law to reflect a human classification. This Maryland law represents the invention of "white" people in law. This moment in history does not reflect a genetic mutation that is linked to a race called "whites"; it represents the need of elites within the colonies to control large masses of laborers, and their desire to have greater access to women.

The Maryland law of 1681 includes the first appearance of the term "white" used to designate a distinct group of humanity in law, and served as a corrective to the antimiscegenation law of 1664 that had the unintended effect of encouraging slaveholders to promote the very marriages the law expressly intended to discourage (*Arch. Md.* 7: 203-205). The law provides that freeborn English or "white" women who enter into marriage with a slave of African descent do so "to the satisfaction of their lascivious and lustful desires" and to the "disgrace not only of the English but also of many other Christian nations" (Ibid. at 204). This language reveals important perceptions and reflects persuasive efforts to shape a human group now being referred to as "white." Taken-for-granted components include that African bodies represent excessive sexuality while bodies seen as "white," like the English, reflect normal sexuality. The normality that is conferred by virtue of one's status as English or white is corrupted and turned sexually deviant by the desire to wed those being constructed as "other" and inferior – first enslaved African men, and then simply Africans. The corruption of the individual is then perceived to harm the group by disgracing the English collectively through challenging what being English symbolizes. The Maryland lawmakers here fuse biology with morality (Battalora 1999: 56). Here criminality is linked not to property damage or physical harm, but to an action that represents a threat to a group status. Here "white" is revealed as fragile, requiring significant protective measures.

The 1681 enactment of the Maryland lawmakers reveals the initial legal authorization of a label and its package of ideas that worked to create, perpetuate, and institutionalize representations of bodies made different, specifically those made "white," and in the most general sense those rendered other-than-white. In addition, the law exposes these community standards to be premised upon a hierarchical ordering of humanity that presupposes the superiority of the English and then reveals the category "English" being expanded to encompass "other whites." We learn here, too, that whiteness was built upon the idea of English *as white* and upon the presumption of the English *as*

Christian. We see also in these enactments that white is reflective of those who are deserving of freedoms and privileges denied those viewed as sufficiently unlike the English. These assumptions and ideas combine in the invention of the new category of humanity.

For those who are now thinking that the invention of white people and the resulting racial hierarchy that follows is the fault of "the damn British," I will caution that such a view of human categorization did not emerge from England and was viewed as peculiar by legal actors there.[20] In England, access to rights and privileges were rooted in wealth, not shades of skin color. It was by British leadership *within the context* of colonial North America that "white" people were imagined and invented. Institutional patterns and commitments within colonial North America include the advancement of a British patriarchy and the development of a capitalist economy dependent upon large numbers of unpaid and/or underpaid laborers. Both of these claims will be elaborated upon in the next chapter.

Discussion questions:

1. What were some names or labels for those who became "white" people before "white" was invented, and why were these problematic?
2. What label other than "white" might have been utilized to divide laborers? What are the possibilities and limitations of the label you suggest?
3. How are workers today divided and separated?
4. When you consider colonial North American laws that represent a break from British common law, what patterns emerge?
5. What threat did Bacon's Rebellion pose to the plantation elite?
6. What were meanings assigned to "white" people from the first creation of them?

CHAPTER 2

Race 101: How "Whites" Became a Success

Naming a group of humanity with a label that sticks is no small feat. It reflects a significant social achievement. In this chapter, labeling is considered through experience and theory. Drawing upon a classroom experiment where some students are labeled in a way to indicate specialness, key components of making a label stick are identified. Next, labeling theory is drawn upon in order to consider the consequences and responses that result from the attachment of a specific label.

Equipped with tools to help us analyze the attachment of a label and the consequences that derive thereby, law as a labeling institution is explored through the imposition of "whites" as a new category of human organization. The series of laws that asserted and imposed "white" people in the decades following Bacon's Rebellion suggest a significant disciplining effort. The laws reveal ties between the invention of "whites" and a distinctly white patriarchal rule. The new human category is shown to be the mechanism by which British elites made a connection with European laborers, in part through a claim of shared authority over "white" women. In addition, it worked to divide laborers into free "whites" on the one hand and enslaved black Africans on the other in support of a slave-based capitalism.

Labeling

I have a classroom of thirty-two students.[21] I announce that the students whose names I call out will hereafter be known as the "pures." I then proceed to read off seventeen student names. I read every other name on my alphabetized roster, and then the last two. No one cares. They think I am silly – perhaps crazy. Next, I separate the students into the "pures" and the rest of the class. I give each group an article that addresses social inequality. The group of pures has an article addressing urban inequality in the U.S. The rest of the class read an article addressing social inequality in Honduras. Each group must respond to the article by critiquing the approach taken by the author to explain the roots of social inequality discussed in the article. When time is up, I have each group submit their written critique.

The critique produced by the pures is much more elaborate, posing questions that challenged the author's assumptions about the organization of society, about group interaction, and about the distribution of power. The critique offered by the other students is minimal and fundamentally lacking in an understanding of Honduran culture and history. I tell the pures that they are special, that they needed to be pulled away from the others so that they are not stifled in their learning. I let the other students know that they are behind and need remedial work. No one complains about the label imposed. The two groups continue to resist the label by failing to use it in our conversations, finding it silly and insignificant.

I meet privately with the "remedial" group and let them know that because they are not adequately prepared, they will face limitations reflected in the grading scheme for the course. I assign homework and explain that the highest grade that they can receive for the assignment is a C, or 75 percent. I explain that it is possible to get below a C, but not higher. Next, I meet privately with the pures and give them their homework assignment. I let them know that the lowest grade a pure can receive on the assignment is a C or 75 percent. A pure can earn an A, but cannot earn a grade lower than a C. Class is over.

When we meet again, I collect homework assignments and divide the groups up into the "pures" and the rest of the class. Students had discussed the grading framework outside of class, and begin to express concern about how the work will be graded. They are claiming that the grading is not fair. For the first time, students are using the label assigned. I move quickly into a discussion of a current event, and show a news clip. I was prepared for such a moment, and am intentional in my effort to distract and engage them in something else. I grade the assignment after class using the different grading scales depending upon the student's group assignment. When we meet again, I return the graded papers and the classroom erupts. Students readily deploy the label assigned and challenge the grading scheme as unfair.

This is a crucial point, because students are utilizing the label assigned. Before concluding the exercise, I have each member of the group of "pures" write up a statement of support for her status as a "pure" and to either support or contest her treatment in the classroom. I then have each member of the remaining group of students address whether he too should be a pure, and why, and then to either support or contest his current treatment in the classroom. These statements are often useful discussion starters. I also ask students the following questions: At what point did the labels assigned begin to matter to you? Why? Are there concerns with the social inequality article assignment and how the article critiques were evaluated? Finally, I have students discuss what it felt like to be in their respective groups.

When we discuss the experience, it becomes clear that no one cared about whatever label I imposed until it came with consequences that I had the perceived authority to implement. The authority to impose consequences that impact lives in concrete ways on the basis of a label makes the label matter. It is also interesting that the more consequences a label packs, the more "real" the label becomes as a matter of experience. Because the label translates into concrete material reality, whether as a resource (such as a grading range from A-C) or a deprivation (such as a grading scale range from C-F), the accumulation of that material reality gives a concrete form to the label, so that those who hold a particular label begin to share certain things and look more alike ("A" students). Some of the "pures" shared that they felt good and special. Some from the other group expressed feelings of anger and the desire to resist the label, the implications of being excluded from it, and the treatment that exclusion brought. Others from that group said they felt bad and inferior. Some "pures" stated that they felt bad because they had a sense that the grading scheme was not fair, though none in the class spoke up.

After processing the experience, I have students identify the key elements of what is required for a label to matter, to become "real" to those upon whom it is thrust and those excluded from it. We deduce from the experience that in order for a label to become "real" it must have consequences that can be readily experienced; the consequences must be such that people generally care about them; the consequences serve to separate some people from others; and these differing consequences are sustained for an adequate amount of time. This exercise in a collective experience of labeling offers important insights that can instruct our consideration of the application of the label "white."

There is a theory within sociology, the sociology of deviance, that is concerned with labels for a "deviant" or "criminal," their successful attachment, and the resulting consequences and responses to the attachment of such a label. This theory was significantly influenced by the work of sociologist Howard Becker. It is called labeling theory, and it is considered to be closely related to interactionist theory.[22] A cornerstone of labeling theory is the idea that deviance is not inherent to an act. Instead, labeling theory focuses attention upon the tendency of majority groups to negatively label minority groups or those viewed as deviating from culturally acceptable norms (Becker 1963). Labeling theory is concerned with how one's sense of self is determined or influenced by the imposition of the "deviant" label, and how one's behavior is determined or influenced by the imposition of the "deviant" label.

The concern of this chapter is to examine the imposition of the human category "white" upon certain people. Therefore, we are concerned with the flip side of the labeling theory coin. Rather than examining a label that constructs a "deviant" or "criminal," we are concerned with a label that renders someone "superior" (via whiteness) to those excluded from the group of humanity. A significant difference is that the label "white" was not imposed by a majority on a minority but, rather, was imposed by a small group of elite lawmakers. These lawmakers had significant power wielding authority upon those who, as a result of the category, combined with the elites to constitute a majority group called "whites." Elites shared little else with other "whites" than the label. Despite the significant differences in the conditions of power that impose a label and the label being one that designates superiority rather than deviance, labeling theory is instructive for the questions and concerns it raises regarding self-identity and behavioral changes that result from the imposition of a label – the self-fulfilling prophecy component. In labeling theory, the self-fulfilling prophecy is one of deviancy. In the exploration of the imposition of the human category "white," the self-fulfilling prophecy is one of superiority.

The student exercise above suggests what is required for making a label stick. The exercise also suggests the import of the subjective and objective experience of being labeled as special (i.e., "pure"). In these ways, the student exercise will inform the exploration of the imposition of the category "white" that follows. From labeling theory, I draw upon the concern with how identity and behavior may be impacted or influenced by the messages that classify and/or describe the group labeled "white." As such, I will highlight the ways in which the first generation of "white" people were organized, separated, and prescribed meaning.

Making White People Real

In the decades following Bacon's Rebellion, colonial Virginia lawmakers utilized law in an extraordinary fashion to constitute "white" people and to discipline all people within the colony into an ideology of whiteness. In other words, these laws worked to promote a set of ideas about reality so as to make it common sense that a person labeled "white" should be in a position of authority relative to a "nonwhite" person. In addition, these laws worked to promote a set of ideas about reality such that those within the group "white" share a commonality based upon that label. In doing so, these ideas rendered "white" culture a taken-for-granted truth.

It should be noted that there was no broad-based evidence of any such mindsets among European laborers at the time of Bacon's Rebellion (1670s). Rather, the evidence is to the contrary. There is no evidence that European laborers conceived of themselves as rulers over their fellow African laborers. The evidence reveals instead that European and African laborers shared a common experience of labor and daily life and, within this context, friendships and joint ventures, including marriage among the European and African laborers ,were neither uncommon nor met with hostility (E. Morgan 1975; P. Morgan 1998; Parent 2003; Smedley 2007).

The set of enactments that Virginia lawmakers passed following Bacon's Rebellion reveal law to be a creative enterprise that literally makes "white" people into a group creating a degree of shared experience and a context that can be called "white" culture. Of course, any time one group is rendered distinct and different, in this case special and superior, the metaphoric coin always has a flip side. In this case, the flip side is the rendering of those excluded from the group as inferior and discardable. The consequences of these extraordinary efforts in law were far-reaching, shaping ideology, constituting social structure, and constructing race. Each will be explored in this chapter.

While Maryland lawmakers were the first to utilize the category "white" to reference a specific group of humanity, it is unlikely that most British and other European laborers within the colonies were impacted or concerned about the invention when it first appeared in 1681. Why? Because the components identified by my students as necessary for a label to stick were not present.

Those women, who the day before the enactment of 1681 were called "British or freeborn," found themselves the day after referenced as "British or other whites" in a law that continued to punish marriage to an enslaved African man. There were no new rewards or punishments for those upon whom the new label was imposed. In other words, the law created no consequences that were unique to the new category of humanity that it invented. It is unlikely that this enactment alone would have produced a successful label, with success being defined as a label that sticks. My students were not concerned that I called them "pures" until the label came with consequences that impacted them in ways they cared about. Similarly, European colonists likely cared little about what lawmakers labeled them when the label came without consequences that they cared about and that were clearly linked to the label.

Bacon's Rebellion remained in everyone's mind. Edmund Morgan notes that "[i]f freemen with disappointed hopes should make common cause with slaves of no hope, the results might be worse than anything Bacon had done. The answer to the problem, obvious if unspoken and only gradually recognized, was racism, to separate dangerous free whites from dangerous slave blacks by a screen of racial contempt" (1975: 328). But the question remained: how to create racism and separation where none yet existed? While there can be little doubt that a concept of the British as separate and distinct from Africans and native peoples existed among lawmakers, a concept of race had yet to be formulated, asserted, and digested, even by elite British in the colonies.

Jacqueline Battalora

In the aftermath of Bacon's Rebellion, Virginia's landowning elite pushed for legislation that established different treatment in law that set "British and other whites" apart from members of native tribes and those of African descent. These laws emerged in the decade following Bacon's Rebellion and continued to build through the first quarter of the eighteenth century, creating consequences that were dramatically different for those labeled "white" from those labeled "negro," "mulatto," or "Indian." The bundle of laws had a dramatic cumulative effect that thoroughly reorganized colonial society.

The package of laws enacted included the prohibition of setting slaves of African descent free and a law making free women of African descent tithable (Hening 1705, 3:87-8; 1668, 2: 267). These laws linked African-ness with a status of servitude. In contrast, parameters and conditions of European labor arrangements of limited bond-servitude were framed by contract law within a corporate context that ensured an agreed-upon termination date extendable only for cause, even if "cause" was loosely interpreted. Another law imposed a prohibition against free blacks holding public office (Hening 1705, 3: 251). Yet another forbade non-Europeans to be owners of Christian bond laborers, with Christian and "white" here overlapping (Hening 1670, 2:280-81). Yet another excluded Africans from the armed militia (Hening 1723, 4: 119). Through such enactments, those of African descent who were established as free members of the colonial community were rendered inferior to both an indentured and non-indentured "white" man. An indentured "white" man held the legal potential of a future position in public office and the ability to own any bond laborer. Through such laws, free people of African descent began to be stripped of the full range of opportunity and resources within colonial society. The messages promulgated by these laws and others include that the privileges of freedom are only fully available to "whites," and that a person of African descent is incapable of being in a position of authority relative to a "white" person.

The laws that prohibited manumission or the freeing of a slave of African descent, that excluded free men of African descent from holding public office, and that prohibited a non-European from owning a Christian bond-laborer, promoted the message that African-ness was positioned below the newly invented group called "whites."

Here the institution of law is exposed as a tool of social reorganization working to put in place a new social hierarchy. The new society would be unlike anything that existed before.

Virginia lawmakers enacted a prohibition against the beating or whipping of a Christian "white" servant while naked without an order from the justice of the peace (Hening 1705, 3:448). This law contrasted with the exclusion of members of native tribes and those of African descent from such requirements, worked to render "white" a special status deserving of protection from humiliation associated with public nakedness and physical punishment. The law began to link "white" with an expectation of due process while denying it to those outside its parameters.

The laws below also contribute to this larger message that "white" people are a special, more deserving group relative to those of African descent. However, the laws that follow had an additional sinister affect. Virginia lawmakers passed an enactment blocking a person of African descent from testifying against a "white" person and another that prohibited free blacks from possessing *any* weapon including a club, gun, powder, or shot, and yet another that subjected a person of African descent to a public lashing for raising a hand against any "white" person (Hening 1705, 3:298; 1732, 4:327, 4:130, 1705, 3:459).[23] These laws combined to render persons of African descent all but completely self-defenseless, especially against violence inflicted by a "white" person. Not only do these laws enforce a human hierarchy that places "white" people at the top, they render the lives of those of African descent less valuable than the most depraved and inhumane "white" person.

Through law, free people of African descent were stripped of the freedoms enjoyed in their status as "free" members of the colonial society. No matter how loyal to the British crown, no matter how faithful to Christianity, no matter how valuable their contribution to the colonial community, people of African descent for the first time faced severe restrictions. They were limited not only in their legal standing within the community, but by virtue of their very ability to preserve and protect their bodily integrity and that of family members. These laws not only exposed free people of African descent to physical harm but worked to exclude African men and African families from the full patriarchal authority afforded under the common law of marriage.

Recalling that under common law the male head of the household was assumed to represent the interests of the family, and expected to provide materially and to *protect* all women, children, and other dependents within the household, the ability of free men of African descent to protect their family members, much less themselves, was severely narrowed by Virginia lawmakers. These laws largely removed these men and their family members from the rights and privileges of patriarchal authority. At the same time, patriarchal authority for "white" men was expanded through antimiscegenation law and through greater free-range over persons of African descent with little regard for civil or criminal punishment.

The law that prohibited a free person of African descent from being in possession of a gun and gunpowder, the law that stripped from African servants their ability to hold and raise livestock, viewed alongside the enactment that listed the required dues owed to a limited-term "white" bond laborer, helps shed light on the material value being attached by law depending upon ones status as "white" or not (Hening1732, 4:327; 1692, 3: 103; 1705, 3:459-60). The freedom dues provided to every "white" male included "ten bushels of corn, thirty shillings in money (or the equivalent in goods), a gun worth at least twenty shillings; and to every woman servant, fifteen bushels of corn, forty shillings in money (or the equivalent in goods)" (Hening 1705, 4:352). These laws combined to render "white" people more valuable relative to those of African descent, whether slave or free. This value or worth attached through judicial action, enforcement, and punishment structures.

Taken as a whole, the laws constitute the scaffolding of a legal structure that served to devalue the dignity and humanity of those seen as other-than-white, in this case those of African descent and sometimes members of native tribes, while inflating that of those seen as "white." It is worth noting that the laws gave European laborers little more than they had before they were "white." A big change that the numerous enactments did create was that "white" people were made better off, not so much than they were prior, but rather in relation to those of African descent and members of native tribes who were made far worse off in the decades following the rebellion. In other words, the laws did little to raise "whites" from their standing prior to Bacon's Rebellion. What the laws did was dramatically lower the bottom through worse conditions and treatment of non-"whites." "White" laborers were given little more than the authority to rule over their fellow laborers of African descent and members of native tribes on the premise that they share a superior status with elites – whiteness.[24]

The inclusion of antimiscegenation law among the series of enactments that created benefits and privileges for "whites" suggests that the law was less of a control mechanism to restrict "whites" than a benefit to them. This claim will be pursued in the section that follows.

The Trade in Women's Bodies

Antimiscegenation law was among the series of enactments passed by Virginia lawmakers in the aftermath of Bacon's Rebellion. Virginia's antimiscegenation law of 1691 was the first to apply its marriage prohibitions to men and women (Hening 3: 453-4). It punished a "white" woman or a "white" man who married a person of African descent or a member of a native tribe by permanently banishing them from the colony. Just a year after the enactment of Virginia's antimiscegenation law, the Maryland Assembly passed legislation prohibiting both "white" women and men from marrying a person of African descent, whether slave or free (*Arch. Md.* 13: 546-549).[25]

Even though the letter of the law restricted both women as well as men, it remained a tool to control largely "white" women's sexuality and relationality, and specifically identified "nonwhite" men. That the law served in this capacity can be shown from the historical roots of the enactment, the statutory language of antimiscegenation laws, and the record of enforcement practices. On its face, the Virginia antimiscegenation law applied equally to men as well as women. While the written law imposed the marriage prohibition upon both "white" men and women, the text of the law addresses only such an infringement by women. Even more telling is evidence of enforcement practices.

Court cases from the antebellum South reveal that antimiscegenation law continued as a legal resource for controlling and punishing largely "white" women who ventured outside of the boundaries of "white" men for sexual and marital relations, while the boundaries for "white" men who engaged in such an illegal relationship were that it be kept casual and discreet. (Bynum 1992; Bardaglio 1995). According to Bynum's study of the antebellum South:

> Magistrates prosecuted primarily white women and black men …White males claimed the right to govern all women, regardless of race. The sole sexual possession of white women by white men assured perpetuation of the dominant "pure" white race (1992: 98-99).

In this way, antimiscegenation law worked to integrally link whiteness with the control of "white" women's and "nonwhite" men's sexuality and relationality.

As part of the legal package of benefits for "whites" that the Virginia lawmakers passed in the aftermath of Bacon's Rebellion, the benefits derived from antimiscegenation law come to light through the emphasis of control within the language of the law and the enforcement practices that followed. From these, we see that the law largely controlled the sexual and marital relations of "white" women and "nonwhite" men, and simultaneously made more women available to "white" men. Such a trade in women's bodies was nothing new.[26]

As moral entrepreneurs, the lawmakers cite British nationhood, Christianity, and the prevention of "abominable beings" as rationale for the law (*Arch. Md.* 1664, 1: 526-527; Hening 1691, 3: 86-88).[27] The law did far more than control the sexuality and relationality of "white" women and nonwhite men. It created a "criminal." Where a child was born, the law created an "abomination." Virginia's antimiscegenation law of 1691 begins by describing children born of a biological parent understood to be English or "white" and a biological parent who was understood as a "negro, mulatto, or Indian" as "that abominable mixture and spurious issue" (Hening 3: 86-88). Through this descriptive alchemy, the general assembly not only worked to create the human category *white* but also a human body anathema to their colonial society. These children were shaped in law as representative of abomination and false descendents.

Virginia's antimiscegenation law required not only that a free English woman who gave birth to a child fathered by a man from one of the prohibited classifications relinquish the child, but also that she pay a fine or face five additional years of servitude (Hening 3: 86-88). In this way, the law served a version of capitalism that relied on nonpaid or underpaid laborers and highlights the sexual vulnerability of women laborers.

The law blocked those relationships between "whites" and those of native tribes or persons of African descent that took an intimate and consensual form from being legitimized by the community and from receiving the protections and exercising the responsibilities created by marriage law. In addition, these laws placed the financial burden, as well as the burden of public shame for "mixed" pregnancies, upon women. "White" men who had children with women understood as not "white" did so largely to the advancement of their investment in property or that of the landowner for whom they labored.

The law that linked a child's status as enslaved or free to the status of the mother legitimized the sexual violation of women of African descent, while antimiscegenation law worked to violate the legitimacy of sexuality for all women. The two laws combined, according to Steve Martinot, to make normative the judicially authorized violation of women's humanity by rendering women instruments (2010, 53). Women of African descent were made capital and thus instruments of wealth production. "White" women were made bearers of "purity" and thus instruments of white supremacy.

Virginia's and Maryland's antimiscegenation laws can be understood as disciplinary measures structuring and enforcing social arrangements, including: establishing a laboring class divided by perceived differences that were being reflected in laws in the early 1660s; furthering a human ordering that presumes the superiority of the British and other Christian Europeans; and reasserting the patriarchal authority of British men and those seen as British-like. Virginia's antimiscegenation law stated, in part:

> …whatsoever English or other white man or woman being free shall intermarry with a negroe, mulatto, or Indian man or woman bond or free, shall within three months after such marriage be banished and removed from this dominion forever, … (Hening 1691, 3: 86-88).

The redefinition of sexuality that antimiscegenation law worked to shape was enforced through banishment from the Virginia colony for life. Banishment reflected the severity of the violation to the new community standards being established. These community standards were being built upon ideas about human difference initiated by lawmakers even before Bacon's Rebellion, but implemented in a manner that would successfully impose this difference following the rebellion through the invention and enforcement of a group of humanity called "whites."

The colonial assemblies of Maryland and Virginia played a significant role in the development of antimiscegenation law and the invention of the human category "white." The Maryland antimiscegenation enactments discussed in chapter one and the Virginia enactment examined here provide a formula for antimiscegenation law that was followed for almost three hundred years in the land that would become the United States: "white" married to "nonwhite" equals abomination. By the late eighteenth century, the prohibition of a "white" person marrying a person of African descent and sometimes various other persons considered not "white" was part of the law of every southern colony as well as that of Massachusetts and Pennsylvania.[28] The pervasiveness of antimiscegenation law reveals how well it served the economic interests of elites and the prevailing gender hierarchy in colonial North America even as it worked to construct new hierarchies.

Through an exploration of post-Bacon's Rebellion enactments of colonial Maryland and Virginia lawmakers, we witness the invention of an entirely new group of humanity, "whites," and the making of a crime, miscegenation. As reviewed in the previous chapter, the first antimiscegenation laws give us a glimpse into the meanings of whiteness. To summarize, they reveal that "white" was derived from the idea of the British as white and Christian. Just as the British were presumed deserving of rights and privileges from which others may be denied, so too were "whites." Just as British represented freedom and purity, so too did "whites."

Gender, from the very first appearance of "white" people in law, produced very different experiences depending upon whether one was male or female. While "white" promised a superiority for all thought to be within its confines, it was never a fulfilled promise for women. For them, white supremacy was enacted in an environment of patriarchal authority and therefore could only be solidified through "white" men.

Meanings assigned to "white" skin were not the same for all people. Rather, the meanings assigned within the four corners (i.e. written words of the document) of the law as well as through enforcement practices took a gendered form. Similarly, the privileges offered to "whites" were not guaranteed absolutely but depended both upon the maintenance of a group or groups understood as "other" (e.g., negroes, mulattos, Indians), and required that individual people rendered "white" remain within the gendered confines of what it meant to be a "white" woman or a "white" man. To the extent that antimiscegenation law worked to embed "white" supremacy in law it did so, in part, through an exchange in "white" women's bodies.

Post-Bacon's Rebellion laws reveal gender, class, and race as interconnected systems that support, constitute, and reconstitute each other – intersectionality at work. Where privilege was created for "whites" through antimiscegenation law it was done, in part, through the reinforcement of a gender hierarchy wherein women were rendered inferior to men. Through this law and its enforcement patterns, privilege on the basis of an emerging "race" called "white" is built in and, through privilege and authority, established on the basis of gender. Where authority over women was secured in marriage through common law, it was denied to a tribal man or a man of African descent relative to a "white" woman. Here, racial constructs are enforced through a granting or denial of the prevailing gender hierarchy.

The fact that laboring Europeans and Africans in Virginia married each other with acceptance prior to the post-Bacon's Rebellion period, and the fact that antimiscegenation law subsequently thrived in excess of three hundred years, helps reflect the dramatic social change that was brought about in the decades following the rebellion. What could bring about such a radical transformation among the laboring classes? It is to a consideration of this change that we will now turn.

Label sticking

The elements that my students identified as necessary for a label to stick include the following: it must have consequences that can be readily experienced; the consequences must be such that people generally care about them; the consequences serve to separate some people from others; and these differing consequences are sustained for an adequate amount of time. The Virginia lawmakers utilized law to create consequences that were readily experienced by bond laborers as well as by those free of servitude. The consequences were not only ones that people generally cared about, influencing quality of life, but consequences that had the potential to impact one's very survival.

Recalling that British, African, and European laborers largely experienced daily life in a similar fashion, these enactments ensured that treatment would become very different soon after their passage. People called "whites" found favorable treatment in law that differed from how these same people were treated prior to the enactments. These same people were not afforded protection from prosecution or liability when the witness(es) to a crime or civil event was of African descent. Nor were those who were rendered "white" forbidden to be beaten naked in public without a court order. Only in and through becoming "white" were they afforded such privileges. Notice that these privileges are only a small improvement from where all laborers stood prior to Bacon's Rebellion.

Law produced consequences that rendered one group of people (whites) the privileged group and other groups of people (most generally, nonwhites) called "negroes," "mulattos," and "Indians," disadvantaged. These laws worked to create a fault line or a gap between laborers that did not previously exist. The fault line was a social separation that can be seen in the colonies beginning in the eighteenth century, and in the United States throughout its history. This separation was not merely linguistic (white and black African or white and Indian) but was reflected in the treatment received as a matter of daily life, creating a dramatic shift from the experience of laborers from Africa and Europe prior to Bacon's Rebellion.

These enactments worked to make "white" people "real" by shaping a range of shared experience and expectation that can be identified as white. The colonial elites had little in common with the European bond laborers who worked for them. With the invention of "white" people they now shared an authority over members of native tribes, and those of African descent built on the promulgation of the idea that they share a superior status – that of whiteness. Here, "race" is working to reconstitute class. The invention also resulted in "white" men sharing an exclusive marital claim to "white" women, while these women were rendered desexualized bearers of white purity. In this way, the invention of "white" people created a bridge that served to unite the ruling elite with large numbers of laborers despite their vastly different social and economic conditions.

Conversely, the invention separated laborers from themselves and each other. The human category "white" worked to alienate "white" women from their own bodies. As previously discussed, the imposition of "white" through antimiscegenation law combined with the law that made the status of a child dependent upon the status of the mother, worked to desexualize "white" women while locating it in the bodies of African women. "White" women were thus constructed as virtuous vessels upon which the "purity" of "whiteness" depended. Sexuality was traded for virtue and the "virtuous woman" became yet another self-concept and group identity that bridged rich and poor through "whiteness."

Despite the greater similarity of laborers' (African and European) social and economic conditions, even after the post-Bacon's Rebellion enactments, the invention of "white" people resulted in a new tier of labor – poor "whites" (Allen 1997, 248-51). This new label allowed "white" laborers to see themselves as more like the plantation elites than the African bodies over whom they now helped rule. Plantation life was reorganized to reflect the different treatment between "whites" and "nonwhites" that the new laws imposed. Poor "whites" emerged as managers over those of African descent and served as the wedge that kept poor "whites" from seeing that their condition was more similar to that of their fellow African and native people than to the elite of the colony. Bacon's Rebellion represented laborers from Africa and Europe united against the landowning elite. "White" people were the solution to that threat.

White as Ideology, Social Structure, and Race

Through the package of laws passed by Virginia lawmakers following Bacon's Rebellion, colonial lawmakers worked to invent the human category "white" and constituted not just rules that constructed a boundary between social order and criminality, but the rules of whiteness (Battalora 1999). These enactments shaped ideology and social structure and help explain the staying power of the fiction called "white" people and their racialization. Each of these claims will be discussed separately.

The term *ideology* means a set of ideas about reality.[29] Sometimes ideology is understood as a way of looking at something that renders it common sense. Let's consider this understanding of ideology in relation to the invention of "white" people in the colonial period. Through a series of laws enacted by Virginia lawmakers from 1691 through 1723, "white" people became a label for people seen as sufficiently like-the-British. A label alone does not constitute an ideology. It is the promulgation of ideas that support action and expectations that is key to ideology. These laws worked to justify the legitimacy of the bondage of persons of African descent and the further exploitation of native tribes by relying upon a way of thinking that viewed English and then simply "white" people as essentially free, as "pure," and as deserving of rights and privileges from which others can be denied.

Let's first begin with the action and expectation that the series of laws direct. Taken as a whole, they instruct all people to see "whites" as more valuable to the community by rendering them, by virtue of legal consequences, literally more valuable. In this way, the social supremacy of "white" people became a fulfilled prophesy for the group. In addition, the laws direct all "white" people to be in a position of authority over those seen as not white. This message of "white" authority, in turn, shaped perceptions of self, group, and others. It would be hard for those labeled "white" to escape at least some level of internalization of the idea that they are better than those seen as not "white," impacting one's sense of self and one's sense of the group to which they are a part. Conversely, it would be equally as unlikely that one could fully escape internalizing the message that those who are not "white" are less valuable. Finally, the laws direct all "white" people to see themselves as a unified group via this value and authority, and through a claim to purity that attached to their status as "white."

The meaning of purity was more than having only "white blood" in one's heritage. The notion of purity that attached to "white" people included an understanding of whiteness as representative of spiritual purity within a Christian context (Ruether 2009: 76). Christian symbolism of light and dark, representing good and evil, readily accommodated transference upon bodies. Christian notions of spiritual purity provided a psychological and socio-political resource for "English or other whites" to shape a moral "Christian" foundation for a hierarchy of humanity that placed "whites" at the top (Battalora 1999: 57-61). Through these laws and with the aid of religious, economic and psychological resources, the idea of "whites" as a superior group became embedded in the minds of people and shaped expectations and goals. Perhaps the strongest and most disturbing evidence of the internalization of such cultural representations of "white" people is the practice of lynching that will be explored later in the book.[30]

If enforcement of the laws passed after Bacon's Rebellion was not enough to impress upon colonists the idea that "white" people are an identifiable group who are essentially different from, in fact superior to, those excluded from the category, then propagandizing efforts imposed by Virginia lawmakers served to clarify. Once each spring and once each fall, parish clerks or churchwardens were required to read in full the laws at the conclusion of Sunday service, while sheriffs were required to do so as well at the courthouse door (Hening 1705, 3:447-62; 1723, 4:126-34). The laws represent a restructuring of colonial society in a way that located all "whites" above Africans and members of native tribes. This restructuring was made common sense through the message that "white" people are superior and ought to be in a position of authority relative to all others, and through laws that imposed such an arrangement.

Ideology alone does not have the staying power that the category "white" has exhibited – some three hundred years. Ideology alone was not the only result of the post-Bacon's Rebellion enactments in Virginia. The laws also constituted *social structure*. Social structure refers to patterned social arrangements that impact individual actions. How did the Virginia laws structure social arrangements and impact individual action? For those who became "white," the classification became valuable for the material, psychological, and spiritual privileges it conferred, even if contingently, while failing to comply with its boundaries was costly.[31] The value and privilege conferred upon "whites" contrasted with the denial of human worth and community privilege for those rendered not "white," and transformed society by dividing laborers who previously were united. Virginia society was reshuffled through these laws to create an entirely new tier of laborers, poor "whites," and an entirely new bottom to the social hierarchy, enslaved persons of African origin and "free" persons of African descent with very narrowed rights of freedom. This new arrangement shaped the actions of laborers in ways that differ sharply from interactions prior to and during Bacon's Rebellion. Those of African descent were rendered passive to the actions of "whites," while "whites" were made managers and rulers. The laws that followed Bacon's Rebellion drove a wedge between "whites" and those labeled other-than-white by creating very different consequences depending upon one's categorization. These different consequences impacted everyday life in profound ways.

In summary, the decades after Bacon's Rebellion saw the simultaneous invention of a group called "whites" and the interpretation and assertion of this group as deserving of rights and privileges from which "others" can be denied. The laws literally made "white" people more valuable by allocating more rights and resources to them, largely by stripping them from those of African descent and members of native tribes. The social structural impact of these laws positioned "white" people both symbolically and materially above (or superior to) those rendered not "white."

According to Omi and Winant, *racial formation* is best understood as a dynamic interaction of both social structure and cultural representation (1994: 56). They explain racial formation as a process or processes "occurring through a linkage between structure and representation" while "racial *projects* do the ideological 'work' of making these links." (Ibid)[32] A racial project is:

> *simultaneously an interpretation, representation, or explanation of racial dynamics, and an effort to reorganize and redistribute resources along particular racial lines.* Racial projects connect what race *means* in a particular discursive practice and the ways in which both social structures and everyday experiences are racially *organized*, based upon that meaning (Ibid.).

This notion of racial project is helpful for our purposes but with a few alterations, since "race" is not yet organized but, rather, being constituted through the post-Bacon Rebellion reorganization of society. The bundle of laws, the meanings they promulgate and the social structure they constitute represent a race-making project. The laws simultaneously represent, interpret and explain an unequal and unfair distribution of resources (i.e., claims to and denial of due process and self defense, possession of a gun, the exercise of political voice in an election) along dividing lines of humanity (i.e., "white" on the one hand and "negro," "mulatto," and "Indian" on the other) that worked to render such groups of humanity "races." As such, the decades after Bacon's Rebellion represent not only the creation of "white" people but the origins of "race," including the "white race."

With this understanding of racial formation, we see the combination of "white" as ideology and "white" as social structure providing the foundation for the construction of "white" people as a racial group. The enactments of the Maryland and Virginia assemblies during the final decades of the seventeenth century and into the eighteenth century reveal the initial legal authorization of a label and its package of ideas that worked to create, perpetuate, and institutionalize representations of bodies made different, specifically, those made "white" and superior in the most general of senses, and those that were not.

Who was "white" was by no means clearly established in the decades following Bacon's Rebellion, and remains undefined as a matter of law to this day. In this way, "white" held the potential to be crafted and contoured by those who held legislative or judicial power, providing them with the ability to include and exclude.[33] An understanding of "white" as ideology and social structure allows for an important distinction to be made. While "whites" references people thought to be so categorized, "whiteness" refers to much more. It is meant to capture not only "white" people, but more so the ideological underpinning that sustains them and the social structures that support the idea of "white" people, what they represent, and their position within society.

A Return to Social Constructionism

British and European colonists did not experience a genetic transformation in the decades following Bacon's Rebellion that turned them from Spanish, Dutch, or British into "whites." The "white race" was no more a biological reality then than it is now. The differences between persons of European and African descent did not emerge from their biological condition, but rather through social enactments that demanded they be treated differently. The series of post-Bacon's Rebellion laws help reveal the role of law in making fiction, the "white race," reality. It did so by constructing or inventing a new group of people called "whites," and it made them "real" by creating very specific consequences and social realities separating those within the category from those without it, through ideology and social structure, giving rise to smoke and mirrors that reflect the appearance of race.

The historical record of the emergence of the human category "white" in law reveals that the category was not inevitable and was not the result of nature, but rather was the result of tremendous human activity. Such human activity included writing and enacting many laws, a regular reading of these laws at church and the courthouse, and strict enforcement. In other words, the human category "white" or the "white race" is a social construct.

Discussion Questions:

1. How did the invention of "white" people serve to unify the relatively few plantation owners with large numbers of British and European laborers, despite their dramatically different economic and social conditions?
2. What social hierarchies facilitated the invention of "white" people, and how did these hierarchies work to render the invention acceptable?
3. What social hierarchies today work to make "acceptable" the split between the one percent of the population who hold the vast amount of wealth in the U.S. from the ninety-nine percent who do not?
4. What role did law play in the making of the "white race"?
5. What creates "white" culture today?

CHAPTER 3

The Americanization of Whites

In the preceding chapters we saw something of when, why, and how
white people were invented. In this chapter and the next, we move
from the colonial era into the first one hundred and fifty years of the
newly formed United States of America. This section will explore the
role of white people as ideology and social structure in organizing the
new republic and shaping its citizenry. In this chapter, foundational
U.S. law and policy regarding immigration and naturalization are
considered. These areas of law are important because they shed light
upon those who have been welcomed into the U.S. and permitted
(by virtue of federal law) to become full participants, and those who
have not. This history continues to influence social interactions in the
twenty-first century U.S. that cause some but not others to be seen as
American.

Historian Ronald Takaki, in chapter one of his book *A Different
Mirror*, lays out the details of what is a familiar experience for him.
While being driven in a taxicab Takaki describes what transpired, in
part, as follows:

My driver and I chatted about the weather and the tourists.
The sky was cloudy, and Virginia Beach was twenty minutes
away. The rearview mirror reflected a white man in his forties.
"How long have you been in this country?" he asked. "All my
life," I replied, wincing. "I was born in the United States."
With a strong Southern drawl, he remarked: "I was wondering
because your English is excellent!" Then, as I had many times
before, I explained: "My grandfather came here from Japan

in the 1880s. My family has been here, in America, for over a hundred years." He glanced at me in the mirror. Somehow I did not look "American" to him; my eyes and complexion looked foreign.

My spouse's parents and numerous aunts and uncles came to this country from Italy. For much of U.S. history Italians who were poor (often from southern regions of Italy) and Catholic were viewed as not white, finding themselves "inbetween" people, a status that will be examined in chapter four. David Roediger describes many new immigrants who held this ambiguous "racial" location before succeeding in becoming white (2005: 119-130). The end of World War Two brought about a fracturing of the prevailing systems of racial rule. As a result, in the decades that followed, these Italians began to be seen as white people. Despite heavy Italian accents, these relatives who arrived in the U.S. in the 1960s are not asked with frequency whether they are visiting or how long they have been in the U.S. They largely experience daily life being treated by bankers, taxi drivers, grocery store cashiers, neighbors, and the like as if they are American. Why? What causes Dr. Takaki to often be viewed as a visitor or newcomer to the U.S.? And why do my spouse's family members experience life as Americans, whether they became citizens or not?

Even words commonly utilized to categorize people reflect a division between Takaki and "American" that does not exist for my spouse's relatives. Takaki often finds himself labeled an Asian American or Japanese American, but rarely do others refer to him as simply American. My spouse's relatives refer to themselves as Italians, but most people refer to them as Americans. Only some have actually naturalized and become U.S. citizens, while others retain their Italian citizenship. They become "Italian Americans" to those with whom they interact when there is a festival or holiday that highlights Italian culture, but for little else. Think about the categories that are available to check off on common governmental, education, or medical forms. Ever seen "Italian American"? How about "Asian"? Why the latter but not the former? How do the available categories work to transform Italians who come to the U.S.? How do they work to transform Japanese who come to the U.S.?

Birth of a White Nation

You may have noticed that quotation marks no longer appear around the word *white* when referring to the group of people so named. I was intentional about doing so in the prior chapters because it helps to highlight white as a construction, an invention of colonial lawmakers. The quotation marks help alert readers to the fact that the word is a recitation or a quote derived from a published text – in this case, colonial law. I am not discontinuing the use of quotations because white is any less of a creation, but in order to reflect the lived reality that the construction worked to shape. Again, no biological or genetic transformations occurred that constituted white people as a distinct group of humanity, much less a race. However, the sustained imposition and acceptance of this fiction called white people resulted in a culture through shared consequences (via social structure) and shared meanings of group, other, and self (via ideology) that worked to form what began to be seen as a race. It should be recognized that ideology and social structure are in dynamic interaction, shaping experience, perception, and expectation. The white race, however fictitious, began in the nineteenth century to be viewed as denoting a biologically distinct human population marked by common phenotypic traits.[34] Indeed, this view is common today despite the fact that no genetic marker has been identified as "white," and despite the fact that more than 99 percent of all genetic markers are shared across so-called "racial" groups.[35]

In the previous two chapters we saw the presumption of superiority that attached to "British and other whites," and the invention of white people as a process with a multitude of influences. The invention was the means by which to divide laborers in the service of a very exploitative capitalism – one increasingly invested in slavery. We also learn from those first laws that white people were presumed to be like the British/Christian, and deserving of rights and privileges from which others can be denied. The package of post-Bacon's Rebellion laws conferred both material and symbolic advantage to whites. Included as part of the value of whiteness for white men was exclusive marital access to white women.

What became racial restrictions on marriage for whites did not end with the colonial era and the American Revolution in 1776. Generally, restrictions (marriage, voting, segregation in schools, work and the military) upon those seen as nonwhite became more numerous as the United States expanded. Antimiscegenation laws became more numerous still after the abolition of slavery in the 1860s.

In this chapter, naturalization law and immigration policy are explored in relation to antimiscegenation laws for what they provide to an understanding of whiteness. Racial restrictions on marriage created all sorts of challenges for immigrants who were classified as other-than-white. Antimiscegenation law, naturalization law and immigration policy combined to severely restrict legitimate relationality and economic advancement for those excluded from whiteness.

Naturalization Law – Patterns and Commitments

In 1790, when the Congress of the United States met for the first time to establish the rules and requirements for immigration and naturalization, the human category white had some one hundred years to spread from Virginia and Maryland and become imbedded within law and society throughout the new republic. Immigration law addresses those persons who seek to come legally into the U.S. from another country. Naturalization law provides the process and guidelines by which one who is not born in the U.S. can become a citizen. Congress in 1790 determined that in order to become a naturalized citizen, one had to be white (Act of March 26, 1790, ch.3, Stat. 103).

The requirement of establishing that one was white for the purpose of naturalization was the law of the land until its repeal in 1952 (8 U.S.C. § 1422).[36] It literally did not matter that one loved the U.S., knew its history, spoke its language, and even fought its wars, if the individual seeking to naturalize could not establish that he or she was white. The case of Mr. Knight is one such example. Discussing the Knight case, Ian F. Haney Lopez in his study of U.S. naturalization law prerequisite cases, provides:

> In 1909, at the age of forty-three, Knight applied for naturalization. He had served in the U.S. Navy for more than a quarter century, receiving a medal in the battle of Manila Bay. Despite his long service to this country…Knight's eligibility to naturalize turned on whether he was a "white person" (1996: 59).

Having a British father and a mother who was half Chinese and half Japanese, it was determined that he was a "half-breed" and therefore, not white (*In re Knight*, 171 F. 299, 300 (E.D.N.Y. 1909)).

Naturalization law, with its requirement that one be white in order to naturalize as a U.S. citizen, was in force for more than one hundred and fifty years. It was modified following the Civil War to include those of African descent (Act of July 14, 1870, ch. 255, § 7, 16 Stat. 254). U.S. naturalization law faced little serious challenge thereafter until World War II when Nazi Germany restricted citizenship to those of the Aryan race, making the U.S. and Germany the only countries with racial restrictions to naturalization (Gordon 1945: 252). The company kept, however, failed to end the requirement of establishing that one is white in order to naturalize as a U.S. citizen.

U.S. naturalization law impacted women differently than men and represents a break from British common law. In England a woman's nationality was unaffected by marriage despite that country's commitment to the common law of coverture. In stark contrast, U.S. law stripped women of their citizenship when they married non-citizen men (act of March 2, 1907, ch. 2534, § 3, 34 Stat. 1228). This termination of women's citizenship was modified in 1922 so that a woman's U.S. citizenship was stripped if she married a non-citizen barred from citizenship because of his race (i.e., not white or not of African descent) (Act of Sept. 22, 1922, ch. 411, § 2, 42 Stat. 1021). These laws that stripped women of their U.S. citizenship were in force until 1931 (Act of March 3, 1931, ch. 442, § 4(a), 46 Stat. 1511).

A consideration of naturalization law in relation to antimiscegenation law reveals the ways in which they combined to work as social control mechanisms and tools of capitalists. This group called "capitalists" is like the plantation elite of the southern colonies, in that they represent the wealthy who exert significant influence over the production and distribution of resources. Naturalization and antimiscegenation law are examined below with an eye toward the patterns that emerge and the commitments that the patterns reveal.

To quickly review antimiscegenation law, it: blocked the social and legal legitimization of a heterosexual relationship between a white and a nonwhite person; worked to direct white women's relationality away from prohibited men and toward white men; and, while the law restricted both white men and women, enforcement was rarely directed toward white men and their nonwhite partners. On the other hand, naturalization law blocked full inclusion of nonwhites into the national and local community while it, like antimiscegenation law, directed women's relational interests away from some men, specifically those who were non-citizens and those excluded from citizenship (i.e., not white), while rendering them more available to others. Antimiscegenation law enforced human difference through the constitution of families made separate and distinct, while naturalization law worked to make communities of people separate and distinct. These laws, in combination with immigration policy, interacted to direct and severely restrict inclusion within the economic, familial, social and political life of the new republic.

Like antimiscegenation law, women and nonwhite men were the emphasis of control via naturalization law. Rather than facing fines, extended years of service, or banishment, nonwhite men and women faced exclusion from full participation in the country and local community via the denial of citizenship and the rights and privileges it confers. Women who were U.S. citizens faced the termination of their citizenship if they did not make a careful marital choice.

Think about why citizenship matters. What does being a citizen get you? Some of the most obvious include mobility into and within the country, employment factors, and participation in the selection of elected representatives. U.S. citizenship enhances mobility into U.S. borders and movement within it. Citizenship increases the ease of employment versus the difficulties or absolute bars to employment when one is in the country seeking employment on a visa, or when one has neither a valid visa or U.S. citizenship. In order to vote, one must be a U.S. citizen. Voting offers people the opportunity to have their interests and concerns brought to the forefront of law and policy. These most obvious benefits of citizenship reveal that it increases access, mobility, and influence. Full citizenship, however, has been described as involving much more.

The easiest and most obvious value of whiteness resulting from this history of naturalization law is directly linked to the value of citizenship. Most basically, citizenship refers to full membership within the community in which one resides and implies a reciprocal exchange of rights in and duties to the community. T.H. Marshall describes full citizenship as having three components: civil, political, and social rights (1964). According to Marshall, civil citizenship consists of those rights that enable individual freedom, such as liberty of the person, freedom of speech and religion, intellectual pursuit, the right to contract and to own property, and the right to justice; political citizenship consists of the right to engage in the political process, either as a member of the political body or an elector of those who make up that body; and finally, social citizenship consists of a wide range of rights including a measure of economic welfare and security, to the right to fully participate in the social heritage and to a civilized life as measured by the prevailing social standards (1964: 78). The social rights of citizenship are required for the exercise of both civil and political rights. In other words, adequate economic and basic social resources including security are necessary in order to be able to vote, run for office or experience individual freedom.

Those denied citizenship via naturalization law faced tremendous disadvantage by being denied the formal or statutory rights of citizenship, much less the substantive rights that Marshall's conception of citizenship captures. Purely formal rights of citizenship include access not only into the borders of the U.S. but to the resources within it. For instance, the lack of citizenship rights created limitations for some groups to organize as laborers, own property, compete for jobs, obtain public services and attain the education and training required to advance in the workplace. Noncitizens excluded from citizenship (i.e., non-whites) were prohibited in eleven states from owning land via the so-called Alien Land Acts, beginning with California's in 1913.

Because whiteness was a prerequisite for citizenship, whiteness was given symbolic and material value as synonymous with U.S. citizenship. While exclusion from formal and substantive rights of citizenship created incredible hardship for the nonwhite noncitizens, it worked to increase the value of whiteness beyond the white equals' American framework. Noncitizens excluded from citizenship (i.e., nonwhite) were denied all but low-wage jobs and difficult conditions. Each exclusion and limitation placed upon nonwhites via the white-only requirement in naturalization law created value for whites, white men in particular, including: access to more land at better prices (via the exclusion of large populations of potential buyers), less competition for skilled jobs, generally more desirable jobs, less competition for advancement within all levels of society, greater access to education and training, and a more influential voice in the body politic.

Much like antimiscegenation law, U.S. naturalization law influenced women's relationality by rendering white male citizens of the U.S. the most "desirable." The 1790 Naturalization Act gave both symbolic and material value to white people. This value was most available to white men and only made secure for white women through white men – in this case, white men who were citizens. In this way, the 1790 Naturalization Act served to advance the commitment to a distinctly white patriarchy. The link between naturalization law and capitalist interests will be explored next with regard to Americans of African, Chinese and Japanese descent.

U.S. Capitalism and White-only Access to Naturalization

Theodore W. Allen, in his detailed historical account *The Invention of the White Race*, does for the human category "white" what Barbara Fields has long called upon us to do: explain race, because race explains nothing. Through the histories Allen tells, he explains the white race as a class concept invented to stabilize and organize Virginia's volatile society by creating "poor white" laborers to manage and oversee bond laborers of African descent. Allen describes the white race that colonists invented as an idea that symbolized cultural and class difference between white laborers on the one hand and African laborers on the other.[37]

We saw in chapters one and two that the invention of white people created a sharp divide in colonial society that did not previously exist, and so required tremendous legal effort and enforcement to accomplish. These efforts and enforcements worked to form an ideology of human difference that made the divide "make sense." That ideology of difference became the ideology of race, of which "white people" were a principal component. Those chapters revealed the inextricable tie between the emergence of white people and the needs and desires of landholding elite to exploit labor as a means of growing wealth. The links between whiteness and capitalist interests are again presented in the assertion of the white-only requirement in naturalization law.

The Naturalization Act of 1790 was drawn upon by those who opposed citizenship for those of African descent. The white-only provision within the Act provided support for the argument that the United States had never considered persons of African descent to be citizens. These arguments were waged within a larger context wherein slavery thrived throughout the south and was racialized black. It must be noted that, while slavery has existed in various places all over the planet and throughout history, not one geographic area or time period wherein slavery was enacted shares a critical feature of the system of slavery that was constructed in the U.S. That feature is the rationalization for enslavement that was rooted in the idea of essential human difference and what "race" categories were deployed to represent and capture.

The *racialization* of those who are of their essence to be free (i.e., whites) and those who are of their essence lazy, prone to criminality, and therefore best suited for enslavement (i.e., black Africans) was a construct of North American slavery and remains one of its legacies. Noel Ignatiev captures the point beautifully: "people from Africa were not enslaved because they were black; rather they were defined as black because they were enslaved" (1995: 186). People from Europe were not superior because they were white; rather they were made white because its promise of superiority placated them as low wage workers.

It is important to remember the body of ethnographic and other historical material that covered the period from the first arrival of laborers from Africa in Virginia through Bacon's Rebellion in 1678. This material suggests that Europeans and Africans understood each other as sharing in a mutual humanity, and these laborers united in a shared struggle for greater opportunity and freedom. There is insufficient evidence suggesting that they viewed each other as separate and distinct human groups. The idea of the black African as essentially lazy and prone to criminality was part of the ideological work of post-Bacon's Rebellion enactments.

The conception of white labor in the north took shape in stark contrast to enslaved labor during the antebellum period. The exclusion of free black people from citizenship worked to render them relatively powerless and to position black people (in both slave and free states) in opposition to white workers, who began to view themselves as "free white labor." The vote was not available to all white men, but in many states depended upon property ownership. David Roediger cites the declining status of black women and men in the early nineteenth century as coinciding with the increased demand for universal suffrage for white men and their identity as "free white men" (1991: 35-36).[38]

U.S. expansion coincided with white workingmen's notions of themselves as independent "free labor," constructed in opposition to nonwhite men and all women who were viewed as dependent and not free. During this time blacks came to be regarded as anathema to American citizenship – as *anticitizens,* and were driven away from Independence Day parades as "defilers" of the body politic. The noncitizenship status of black Americans was ultimately decided in 1857 when the U.S. Supreme Court ruled in *Dred Scott* that blacks had never been citizens and therefore could never be citizens, finding that even emancipated blacks were not part of "the people" brought into existence via the U.S. Constitution and therefore can claim none of the rights and privileges derived there from (*Dred Scott v. Sandford*, 60 U.S. (19 How.) 393 (1857)).

Black Africans were seen as a potential resource of the rich that could be deployed to advance their interests. As persons of African descent were rendered more powerless, the threat they presented became greater. Persons of African descent were seen as pawns of capitalists, and as such, a continual threat to the freedom of white laborers.[39]

It was not until the enforcement of post-Civil War amendments that black Americans were afforded formal citizenship. During the brief period of federal Reconstruction, when federal troops and judges were sent to the former slave states, black Americans experienced many of the rights of citizenship. With the onset of a weaker economy, support for black civil rights waned and federal Reconstruction ended, and with it the exercise of formal citizenship for Americans of African descent.[40]

The civil rights laws became nullified by lack of enforcement by local authorities, and practices took hold that drew sharp divides along lines seen as racial. For example, after 1890, racially segregated residential areas emerged as a result of increased anti-immigrant sentiment and white political action (Delaney 1998: 125-178; Massey and Denton 1993: 30-35). These practices reigned in the era of American apartheid (also referred to as Jim Crow) and were given the constitutional stamp of authority in 1896 by the Supreme Court decision *Plessy v. Ferguson*, 163 U.S. 537 (1896). These events helped ensure that black men and, after 1920, black women would be denied the vote and almost every other experience and expression of citizenship rights until the Civil Rights Movement of the 1950s and 1960s.[41]

Black Americans were not the only group excluded from citizenship, rendered as cheap labor, and viewed as peripheral to the opportunities and resources of America with the aid of naturalization law. For much of the late nineteenth and early twentieth centuries, naturalization law, with its white-only requirement, worked to maintain an abundant supply of dependent, cheap labor via the bodies of Chinese and then Japanese laborers. According to Evelyn Nakano Glenn, the noncitizen status of Chinese and Japanese laborers ensured by naturalization law "helped mitigate one potential problem for the (Hawaiian sugar) planters: how to ensure an abundant supply of labor and at the same time retain their (the planters') political dominance despite their small numbers" (2002: 203). The latter was accomplished through disenfranchisement and disenfranchisement was accomplished by the 1790 Naturalization Act.[42]

Because naturalization was rendered a white-only process, and because exclusion from citizenship worked to supply capitalists with a ready source of cheap labor, it becomes difficult to pull apart the commitment to exploitative capitalism from whiteness. The 1790 Naturalization Act is a statement about who is considered a "real American" and reveals that in the Unites States, white people are not only the most welcome but the most valued. This does not mean that some white people did not work hard or that they did not face hardships. One does not preclude the other. What laws like the 1790 Naturalization Act reveal is that the playing field upon which people came to the U.S. to labor, have a family, and prosper was anything but equal, and that a significant determinant of the degree of difficulty one faced turned on whether the person was white or not.

The lines that created greater or lesser ease upon this playing field were determined significantly by ideas about human organization called race, of which white and black served as polar opposites. The social construct called "race" cannot be overemphasized in understanding the organization of U.S. society from its formation. The understanding of whites as superior and blacks stereotyped to a caricature known as "the nigger" seen as lazy, prone to criminality, and unworthy of respect or fair treatment reflected the social divide. Anthropologist Audrey Smedley explains:

> Once reified, that is, crystallized and rendered as substantive reality, the folk idea of race assumed an identity and autonomy of its own, aided by the authority of learned opinion. The autonomy of any aspect of culture is, of course, relative. But ideas and ideologies, when institutionalized in people's minds, often develop a fluidity and refractivity that allow them to persist even in drastically altered situations. In this case, the amorphous nature of race meant that the ideology could transcend the sources of its origin, and race classifications could be logically extended to any populations where inequality and a sense of unbridgeable differenced were desirable. Such populations could be identified by color or other physical features, and their relative ranks established accordingly (2007: 225).

While the social polarization of white people and black Africans serves as the "basic ingredients out of which the ideology of race was most visibly generated, it is clear that other peoples also could be racialized and fitted into the scheme. Wherever there were visible physical and/ or cultural differences among new immigrants to the United States, the potential for the stigma of racial inferiority could be, and usually was, applied."[43]

Consistent with the invention of white people in the aftermath of Bacon's Rebellion, where the invention of whites served as the mechanism to divide laborers in the service of capitalism, the two commitments, whiteness and capitalist exploitation, are revealed as merged in the U.S. context, reflecting two sides of the same coin. This was by no means inevitable. There are many ways to divide and separate people, and many ways to exploit labor. In colonial North America and then the United States, white people have served this purpose.

Immigration and the Making of the "Native American"

The expansion of U.S. land holdings and industrialization worked to fuel capitalist ventures and the demand for cheap labor. President Abraham Lincoln, in his 1863 message to Congress, urged them to establish a system that would encourage immigration, noting that there was a "great deficiency of laborers in every field of industry."[44] Laborers were sought to work fields and mines, construct the railroad and, as industrialization advanced, work in the factories. China and Ireland provided a ready supply of poor laborers willing to come toil in the U.S. Immigration laws from the nineteenth century into the twentieth century were shaped by a number of often competing forces, including U.S. expansionism, manifest destiny, nativism, and industrialization. The expansion of U.S. land holdings and the ideology of manifest destiny will be explored in the next chapter.

Prior to 1830, most white immigrants to the U.S were Protestants from England or other parts of Europe. In the decades that followed, the faces and identities of those new to America changed to include: Catholic immigrants, especially those from Ireland in the face of a potato famine; Mexicans, many of whom were Catholic, who found themselves after the signing of the Treaty of Guadalupe Hidalgo living in the U.S.; and men from China and then Japan who were sought by capitalists on the west coast. In addition, the sheer numbers of those coming to the U.S. rose significantly.[45]

That so many immigrants in this wave were construed as not white, including the Irish, southern Italians, Polish, and Greeks among others, worked to feed the anti-immigrant or nativist sentiment that was being articulated. John Higham defines nativism as extreme opposition to a minority within national borders based upon that minority's foreign (i.e., un-American) connections (1955: 4-5). Nativism sharpened the understanding of Americans as those who are Anglo-Saxon and Protestant. In fact, white Anglo-Saxon Protestants came to be seen as "native Americans" in opposition to the droves of non-white (many of whom later became white), non-Protestant immigrants who came to the U.S.[46]

Nativism manifested in many ways, but none more clearly than through the passage of immigration exclusion acts, or laws that blocked people from certain countries from legally emigrating to the U.S. These laws are particularly interesting because they reveal who was seen as a threat to American life. Conversely, immigration exclusion acts also help sharpen those seen as American. In addition, immigration exclusion laws reflect the conflict between laborers and capitalists, or those who own and control the mode of production and are always seeking cheap labor. This conflict is most often manifested as competition among workers rather than as exploitation on the part of the latter.

The welcome that the U.S. had historically shown to European immigrants was extended to Chinese in the interest of rapid economic development in the west after gold was discovered in California in 1848. U.S. immigration law admitted only Chinese men. Antimiscegenation laws in places where Chinese populations were sizable included the prohibition of whites marrying Chinese. These laws combined to severely limit the ability of Chinese men in the U.S. to form families, making the primary means of patriarchal authority largely unavailable. These laws also created an underground market in Chinese women's bodies. Chinese prostitution flourished where significant numbers of Chinese male laborers lived and worked, and became a resource for nativists and others to claim that Chinese were heathens.

The ideology of "free labor" that took shape in the antebellum north transformed into the white workingmen's campaign for a "man's wage" by the Progressive era (1890s-1920s). A man's wage was an amount sufficient to support a male laborer and his family at a respectable standard. This idea of an appropriate wage grew out of the reorganization of work and gender roles that occurred in the nineteenth century as a result of industrialization. The mechanization of work drew a wedge between the home, seen as a private realm, and work, seen as a public realm. Prior to industrialization, the home and the land constituted the location of work with tremendous overlap in work performed my women and men (with the exception of work circumscribed by human reproduction). With the onset of industrialization, work was increasingly performed away from home within a factory and by men. The call for a man's wage had both racial and gender dimensions.[47]

According to Alice Kessler-Harris, a working white woman's wage was viewed as supplemental regardless of her situation and, as such, calculated at a low rate and deemed not necessary for family well-being (1990: 8-9). On the other hand, black, Mexican, and other nonwhite women were viewed as laborers in part because they were excluded from the ideal gender ideology that constructed (white) women as virtuous, having pure morals, and excelling at activities in domesticity, including the rearing and education of children. While white women's wages were justified as lower relative to men, nonwhite women's wages were justified as lower than white women's on the basis that nonwhite people's standard of living was presumed to be lower than that of white Americans. Similarly, a "man's wage" did not apply to nonwhite men who were excluded from such claims to patriarchal authority through the feminization of their work as unfree, the rendering of their work "dirty" and therefore unfit for whites, and the belief by whites that nonwhites could survive on next to nothing.[48]

For example, a 1902 survey of Hawaiian plantations showed that American (white) workers doing equivalent work were paid an average of $3.82 a day, Portuguese $2.61, Native Hawaiian $2.12, and Japanese $1.63. White overseers were paid 57 percent more than Portuguese overseers and 100 percent more than Japanese. This wage stratification continued in 1915, when another survey was conducted.[49]

Just as nonwhite men were excluded from inclusion within the construct of free labor, they were excluded from newly emerging expressions of patriarchal authority via a "man's wage." The ideal of a man's wage rendered female dependence upon male support a prerequisite in order for men to be real men. Furthermore, exclusion from the gender ideals of masculinity worked to feminize and, as a result, to denigrate nonwhite men.

Jacqueline Battalora

White workingmen's efforts to advance their position included efforts to exclude nonwhite men as competitors. These efforts manifested not simply in lower wages for Chinese laborers, but taxes and exclusion from buying land and testifying against a white person, among others. Chinese miners were forced to pay a tax pursuant to the 1850 "Foreign Miner's Tax" that was imposed upon those who were not "native" (born in the U.S.) or naturalized citizens. Then, in 1862, the Chinese had to pay a "police tax" of $2.50 a month. The California Supreme Court, in the 1854 case *People v. Hall*, held that Chinese and all other nonwhite people are prohibited from testifying against whites (4 Cal. 399 (1854)). Some efforts to exclude Chinese often ran counter to the continued demand for cheap labor on the part of capitalists and other large employers, as in the 1862 California law titled, "An Act to Protect Free White Labor Against Competition with Chinese Coolie Labor, and to Discourage the Immigration of the Chinese in the State of California."[50]

It should be noted that each of these taxes and restrictions served to advance the value of whiteness. White workers not only received higher wages but could retain more of them, simply by virtue of their whiteness that gave access to citizenship. Alexander Saxton explains that most of the country suffered significantly during the depression of the mid-1870s due in no small part to the completion of the railroad that left many out of work (1990: 294-296). Economic hardship worked to escalate racial and political tensions that pre-existed the economic downturn and gave a greater voice to nativist sentiment. Railroad strikes on the east coast sought to address cuts in wages and increased workloads. "They erupted into mass insurgency against government seemingly favorable to the interests of industrial entrepreneurs at the expense of working people" (Ibid at 297). There were uprisings in cities across the country, including San Francisco, where demonstrations in support of railroad strikes were taken over by anti-Chinese agitators who killed Chinese in the streets. "Anger at the Central Pacific Railroad was transposed into violence against Chinese, of whom the railroad was reputedly the largest employer."[51]

The formula that has been repeated numerous times in U.S. history – economic recession, increased unemployment, and a group of laborers seen as not white and not American who serve as the explanation for other laborers' difficulties – worked in this case to galvanize anti-Chinese sentiment into national legislation. Congress in 1882 passed the Chinese Exclusion Act (ch. 126, 22 Stat. 58 (1882)).[52] For the first time, the nation's traditionally open immigration policy was altered, and did so by imposing a restriction upon a single group – Chinese laborers. The demand for cheap labor by manufacturers of consumer goods and entrepreneurs, however, did not cease, and the success of the Chinese in serving as cheap and controllable labor was not lost on them. Chinese laborers had been rendered relatively powerless. They were politically powerless thanks to naturalization law and therefore very much under the control of those for whom they labored. They were rendered largely single via antimiscegenation law and a men-only immigration policy, and therefore excluded from patriarchal authority exercised in and through the family.

For a supply of cheap labor, companies and landowners would next turn to Japan and Mexico. The migration of people from these two countries began to increase significantly by the 1890s. The result, according to Saxton, is that "preserving the West as a white man's country would thus remain for another seventy-five years central to labor organization and working-class politics" (1990: 300). The Chinese Exclusion Act represented this movement's success, as it was endorsed by popular majorities in western states and received bipartisan congressional approval.

The success of those advocating nativist sentiment galvanized opposition to the Japanese laborers who were rendered by laws, much like the Chinese, as cheap and dependent labor. In 1907 a Gentleman's Agreement was entered into with Japan, under which the Japanese government agreed not to issue passports to emigrants to the United States except for certain business and professional men. In exchange, President Theodore Roosevelt pressured San Francisco to rescind the order segregating Japanese American children from white children within schools there. Capitalists turned to the Philippines.[53]

Broad sweeping exclusion followed. "Concern over these foreign elements led to the organization, by a group of Harvard alumni, of the Immigration Restriction League in 1894. The platform of this and other such organizations aimed to restructure immigration policy solely on racial grounds. As is well known, by 1924, they were eminently successful in lobbying for immigration restrictions."

Congress passed the National Origins Act, or the Johnson-Reid Act of 1924, that resulted in a more complete exclusion of Japanese among other groups. The Act halted "undesirable" immigration by quotas and barred specific groups from the Asia-Pacific Triangle.[54]

Here we see whiteness, in the form of the 1790 Naturalization Act, used as the mechanism to exclude from the U.S. those from Japan, China, the Philippines (then under U.S. control), Laos, Siam (Thailand), Cambodia, Singapore (then a British colony), Korea, Vietnam, Indonesia, Burma (Myanmar), India, Ceylon (Sri Lanka) and Malaysia. Those prohibited from naturalizing via the 1790 Naturalization Act were prevented from immigrating to the U.S. by the National Origins Act of 1924. Because these first restrictions upon immigration to the U.S. focused upon control of people from Asia, they served as the model for future anti-immigrant rhetoric and policy. For example, immigrants thereafter, regardless of their country of origin, were often referred to as "Orientals."[55]

Nativism in the U.S. during the nineteenth century was itself an expression of whiteness combined with class and religious bigotry and fear of degraded working conditions. The movement sharpened the divide between white Anglo-Saxon Protestants, who were seen as native Americans, and all others, who were neither.

Law and Whiteness

Immigration and naturalization law deployed whiteness as the means to more sharply define who was American and who was a "real American" regardless of citizenship, as we will see more clearly in the following chapter. At the same time, they advanced this invented group of humanity called whites by asserting them in law, and as a result, assigning significant meaning and value to whiteness as a matter of national law and policy. This value manifested within the social structure, not only in access to formal citizenship and greater ability to immigrate to the U.S., but through greater access to the political, civil and social rights of citizenship.

White ideology was built from the idea of those deemed sufficiently like the British, and has shaped U.S. history in profound ways. It has constructed "American" as consistent with white. It has worked to commodify women's bodies in racialized ways: white women as those who must preserve white purity; and nonwhite women as sex slaves, laborers at the bottom rung of the pay scale, and defective women by exclusion from idealized gender roles. Whiteness has centered patriarchal authority and power in the hands of white men.

From the invention of white people in the late eighteenth century, whiteness has served as a tool for supporting the interests of capitalists. Whiteness, through its ideological and social structural influences, has worked to define labor struggles by focusing attention and blame on nonwhites as the cause of poor working conditions or low wages, and away from the capitalists whose policies and practices most significantly impact conditions and wages. Whiteness has promulgated fundamental inequalities that keep the U.S. from fulfilling some of the most fundamental ideals it espouses: equal opportunity and liberty for all.

As Ian F. Haney Lopez explains, "the racial composition of the U.S. citizenry reflects in part the accident of world migration patterns. More than this, however, it reflects the conscious design of U.S. immigration and naturalization laws" (1996: 37). Of course, the racial composition of U.S. citizenry also reflects U.S. expansion and relational patterns. It should be highlighted here that the design of the U.S., reflected in part through immigration, naturalization, and expansion, is significantly guided by an ideology of whiteness, including that white equals American.

I have focused thus far on three areas of law – antimiscegenation, naturalization, and immigration – to explore the creation and meanings of whiteness and to reflect upon the patterns they shape and the commitments they reveal. Each of these areas was transformed legally in the 1950s and 1960s but their footprint has yet to be removed from the landscape of interpersonal relations, political action, the organization of communities, and racial ideas, not the least of which is that "white" constitutes a race.

The everyday experiences of Dr. Ronald Takaki (which reveal he is viewed by many as not American) versus those of my spouse's Italian family members expose that in the twenty-first century U.S., being seen as white continues to impact whether or not one is viewed and treated as American. Dr. Takaki and others of Japanese descent remain outside of the current construct of white, while Italians in the

U.S. have been folded into it. Because immigration and naturalization law and policy have worked to create a "white equals American" equation, those who are viewed as white are likely to be likewise viewed as American. This history reveals that being seen as American has had little to do with how long one's family has been in the U.S. or how much one's family has contributed to the educational, business, military or any other success the U.S. can claim.

So far we have considered a slice of African American, Chinese, and Japanese experience in the U.S. through the lens of naturalization and immigration law, and with attention to whiteness. All three groups have been and remain firmly excluded from the human category called white. They were excluded as a matter of law for purposes of citizenship, and excluded as a matter of everyday social interactions.

The groups to whom we now turn have had a very different experience in relation to whiteness. We will look at a group that was rendered white for the purpose of naturalization and antimiscegenation laws but not white for anything else, and a group that was rendered inbetweeen people before firmly establishing their status as white – Mexican people who found themselves living in the U.S after the signing of the Treaty of Guadalupe Hidalgo and Irish immigrants of the nineteenth century will be examined for a greater understanding of whiteness, its meanings and workings in U.S. law and society.

Discussion Questions:

1. In what ways did the group of humanity called "whites" determine or shape social, economic, and political institutions and practices?
2. In what ways was whiteness rendered symbolically valuable? In what ways was whiteness rendered materially valuable?
3. Can you identify the footprints of this history in current U.S. society, policy, and/or practices?
4. How has this history worked to shape and organize families and communities today?

CHAPTER 4

Contingent Whites and Inbetween People:
Mexicans and Irish in the U.S.

In colonial North America, the plantation elite used law to create, impose, and enforce white people. The invention separated workers who were previously united in opposition to large landholders, and united people previously divided by starkly contrasting economic and social conditions. The divisions and allegiances that the invention of white people forged reorganized colonial society and, as we saw in the previous chapter, significantly organized the new republic. By the nineteenth century, new ideologies were promulgated that reasserted old tools, including whiteness, in the service of capitalist interests. One such ideology came to be called Manifest Destiny, and is integrally tied with U.S. expansionist efforts. Nativism was another, and was significant in shaping not only U.S. immigration policy, but the national political terrain.

In this chapter, we will examine U.S. expansionism and whiteness through the experience of Mexicans in the U.S. following the Treaty of Guadalupe Hidalgo, and nativism and whiteness through the experience of Irish Catholics in the mid-nineteenth century U.S. The two groups allow for an exploration of various not-really but sort-of-white statuses and, as such, expose the struggle over who defines white, and the very struggles and opportunities that whiteness presented.

Mexicans in the U.S. were determined to be white by law as a result of international treaties, and yet were repeatedly refused inclusion within and the benefits of this status. As a result they were rendered what I call "contingent whites," because the only benefits of whiteness received were those conferred explicitly by federal law that required the status white (i.e., naturalization law). The Irish who came in large numbers after the first quarter of the nineteenth century provide an example of what John Higham and Robert Ortis have called "inbetween peoples." David Roediger explains this as the status of certain new immigrants to the U.S. who fell inbetween "hard racism and full inclusion – neither securely white nor nonwhite..."[56]

As a matter of federal law, Mexicans were white and therefore could not be excluded from naturalizing. State law, however, was another matter. Almost every state with a significant Mexican population excluded them from the status "white" for the purposes of state laws with the exception of one area, antimiscegenation law. Rather than experiencing life in the U.S. as those who were understood to be white, Mexicans were rendered "unfree labor," excluded from a "man's wage," blamed for low wages and poor working conditions, and excluded from almost every benefit of their federal legal status as white.

The history reviewed in chapters one and two suggests that law played a significant role in the invention of white people, not only in the assertion of the label and the group but also in the imposition and enforcement of its meanings. Why did being labeled white by virtue of international treaties fail to confer upon Mexicans and Mexican Americans the status as a matter of state law and general social practice? This question is pursued in this chapter.

Exclusion from citizenship via the white-only requirement in naturalization law was a key factor in the exclusion of Chinese and Japanese, among others, from many rights and opportunities available to whites. The means of exclusion from these rights and opportunities for Mexicans was different. Rather than being excluded from naturalizing because access to citizenship was rendered a white-only process and Chinese and then Japanese were rendered not white, Mexicans were given access to citizenship via a U.S. treaty with Mexico. However, neither access to formal citizenship nor the rendering of Mexicans white by virtue of federal law managed to secure this status and its benefits as a matter of social practice and even law in most states. The evidence reveals that Mexicans were instead interpreted to be not "really" white.

U.S. Expansionism and the Mexican-American War

Rodolfo F. Acuna locates the roots of the Mexican-American War back in 1767, when Benjamin Franklin identified Mexico and Cuba for future U.S. expansion (2007). Actions in furtherance of this desire began with the organization of white Americans to engage in insurrectionist activity through expeditions into Mexico (Texas) beginning in the 1790s. These efforts were fueled by a number of expansionist successes, including the Louisiana Purchase of 1803 and the Adam-Onis or Transcontinental Treaty of 1819, which followed the invasion by U.S. troops into Florida and resulted in Spain ceding that state to the U.S.[57]

Expansionism was a pervasive idea in U.S. culture prior to the mid-nineteenth century. John O'Sullivan, editor of the *Democratic Review*, created the term "Manifest Destiny" and was influential in shaping public opinion and motivations for U.S. expansion. Manifest Destiny is a religious doctrine with Puritan roots that holds that the U.S. reflects the chosen people predestined for salvation. Newspapers and political speeches promoted expansion, as well as national intellectuals including Walt Whitman and Ralph Waldo Emerson, and politicians including John Quincy Adams and Andrew Jackson. The newspaper editor O'Sullivan claimed that it was America's "destiny to overspread the whole North American continent with an immense democratic population," and that white Americans would spread democracy and freedom to lesser peoples in the process.[58]

The desire for land backed by a moral directive to spread the principles of democracy and Protestant Christianity led the U.S. Congress to almost unanimous support of a declaration of war against Mexico in May of 1846. After the war, Mexico was forced to cede one-third of its territory, the northern part, to the United States for a sum of $15 million. This vast expanse of land includes what are now the states of California, New Mexico, Arizona, Nevada, Utah, Texas, and part of Colorado, and encompassed some 100,000 Mexican citizens, including a variety of native tribes such as Navajo, Apache, Pueblo, and Comanche.[59]

Imagine how extraordinary this time must have been. Mexican citizens found themselves living within and owning land in a new nation without having moved. How did the treaty affect their citizenship? How did it impact land grants? These were key features of the Treaty of Guadalupe Hidalgo and areas of great concern to the Mexican leadership. The U.S. Senate ratified the treaty but deleted Article X, which dealt with explicit protection of Mexican land grants, specifically those in Texas. Only Articles VIII and IX remained with a promise of protection for private property. Article IX of the treaty provides in part:

> Mexicans....shall be incorporated into the Union of the United States, and admitted at the proper time (to be judged of by the Congress of the United States) to the enjoyment of all the rights of citizens of the United States according to the principles of the Constitution; and in the mean time shall be maintained and protected in the free enjoyment of their liberty and property, and secured in the free exercise of their religion without restriction.[60]

According to Article VIII, Mexicans who elect to remain in the U.S. may either "retain the title and rights of Mexican citizens, or acquire those of citizens of the United States." Those who failed to make the election to remain a Mexican citizen within one year, the Article provides, "shall be considered to have elected to become citizens of the United States." Article VIII goes on to provide that Mexican property shall be respected providing, "present owners, the heirs of these, and all Mexicans who may hereafter acquire said property by contract, shall enjoy with respect to it, guaranties equally ample as if the same belonged to citizens of the United States."[61]

Mexican opposition to ratification provides some international perspective with regard to existing racial hierarchies in the U.S. Mexican diplomat Manuel Crescion Rejon expressed his reservations about the impending treatment of Mexicans in the U.S., stating:

> Our race, our unfortunate people will have to wander in search of hospitality in a strange land, only to be rejected later. Descendants of the Indians that we are, the North Americans hate us, their spokesmen depreciate us, even if they recognize the justice of our cause, and they consider us unworthy to form

with them one nation and one society, they clearly manifest that their future expansion begins with the territory that they take from us and pushing [sic] aside our citizens who inhabit the land.[62]

Rejon's fears for Mexicans in the U.S. were proven to be valid. Violation of the treaty occurred almost immediately. Mexicans lost their land and many, including those who were members of native tribes, were denied the promise of U.S. citizenship.

The American legal system became an instrument by which Mexicans lost their land and were displaced. The U.S. landowning system is based upon legal title. In this system, land is individually owned and can be subdivided and sold without regard to heirs. The Mexican system of landowning was rooted in tradition and considered a patrimony, residing ownership in family lines, not individuals. In addition, it included communal land grants that provided rights of use such as for grazing or farming. These latter grants were not recognized under U.S. law, and the lands were simply taken and sold to white speculators and businessmen.[63]

The transformation of the landowning system for Mexicans resulted in many native landowners losing land. In 1850 more than 60 percent of Mexican households owned land in the U.S. valued at more than one hundred dollars. Ten years later, that number declined to only 29 percent. Land commissions were set up in order to review claims to ownership by Mexicans. In California, the commission required even those holding perfected title to have ownership approved. In the process of trying to validate their claims to the land under U.S. law, many Mexican landowners lost land, not because of defective title but as a result of excessive legal fees to American lawyers. Those failing to bring their claim to ownership within a specified period of time were deemed to have abandoned their title. Others lost land through fraud, legal chicanery, land seizure due to failure to pay taxes, or through lynching and other violence. A few less than six hundred Mexicans were lynched in the United States between 1848 and 1928. Most were executed by mobs.[64]

What was secured for Mexicans in the U.S., at least initially, was their status as white by virtue of federal law. The Treaty of Guadalupe

Hidalgo and other treaties designated Mexicans legally as white. This was confirmed by the naturalization case *In re Rodriguez,* wherein the court granted citizenship not because the Texas federal court believed a "pure-blood" Mexican was white, but because a series of treaties including the Treaty of Guadalupe Hidalgo (1848) and the Transcontinental Treaty (1819) conferred citizenship on Mexicans and Spaniards (81 F. 337 (W.D. Tex. 1897) 349-354). The law imposed a white status, despite the perception of legal actors that this was not "true." The U.S. Department of Labor in the 1920s wrote, in reply to a request from those advocating a eugenics perspective and seeking to challenge the *Rodriguez* decision, that the U.S. "Government, in its relations with the Mexican people, has uniformly recognized them as belonging to the white race."[65]

Mexicans were provided access to citizenship through the Treaty and were not blocked from naturalizing because of the white-only requirement, because naturalization law was and remains a process under the jurisdiction of the federal government, not the states. However, they were not white for purposes of much else. There were definite limits to the share in whiteness that Mexicans experienced, both as a matter of ideology and social structure. For example, Mexicans faced many of the exclusions experienced by those of African and Chinese descent in the U.S. Recalling that in 1850 California prohibited Chinese and Native Americans from testifying against whites, this law was later used to prohibit Mexicans as well. For example, Manuel Dominguez, a signatory to the first constitution of California and a wealthy landowner and county supervisor, had his testimony barred (*People v. Elyea*, 14 Cal 145 1859).[66]

During the mid-nineteenth century, most whites made racial distinctions regarding Mexicans on the basis of class and appearance. Whites accepted the Spanish heritage of those with significant landholdings, thereby recognizing them as a type of white person. Here we see the meaning of white conflated with wealth. For the majority of Mexicans who were small farmers, herders, and workers, this was not the case. Instead, whites considered them variously as Indian, mestizo, or otherwise like black persons of African descent. These constructs of Mexicans placed them squarely in the category of "unfree" labor and therefore "properly" excluded them from the full range of rights of American citizenship.[67]

By the early twentieth century, even elite Mexicans began to be viewed as not white. "A Texas Congressman noted in 1920, 'We use the term Mexican to designate a race, not a citizen or subject of the nation.' When queried about the race of Mexicans, a Chicago Chamber of Commerce official responded: 'No they are not regarded as colored, but they are regarded as an inferior class. Are Mexicans regarded as white? Oh no!'" Evelyn Nakano Glenn explains the process of Mexican racialization as rooted within the struggles over Mexican labor and citizenship.[68] It should not be missed that those struggles arose in no insignificant part because of the white race – what it had come to represent and how it was enacted.

Many non-Mexican whites refused to recognize them as Americans entitled to political and civil rights. Mexicans were often denied entry to public facilities designated for "whites only." The denial of so many rights of citizenship rendered Mexicans cheap and dependant labor. For example, in 1908 Mexican miners were paid two dollars a day while white workers were paid three to five dollars a day. California growers preferred Mexicans to white workers precisely because they could pay them less. A grower noted that Mexicans should be paid only enough to sustain themselves, with a dollar or two to spend.[69]

They were viewed as aliens whether born in the U.S. or Mexico. As a result, they were questioned as to their status as American citizens, especially when they sought to exercise political rights. In fact, by the late 1880s Populists and Republicans campaigned for stripping all Mexicans of the right to vote. While Populists challenged the expansion of agribusiness and sought reforms in government, they blamed Mexicans for the demise of small farms. This is, of course, is a pattern we have seen before – focus upon a not white or, in this case, not fully white group, as the cause of labor problems, rather than the social structures that condition the problems and the capitalists who control the conditions and wages of labor.[70]

Being white by law permitted Mexican inclusion into whiteness for the purposes of antimiscegenation law. However, as we have seen, Mexicans were excluded from whiteness for the purpose of: testifying against a white person; the assignment of wages; inclusion within "free white labor" and claims of a "man's wage;" and the many other civil, political and social rights of citizenship. Treaties explain how Mexicans were viewed as white for the purpose of such federal laws as naturalization. What might explain the inclusion of Mexicans into the category white for the purpose of antimiscegenation that was state law, but for little if anything else as a matter of law in those very states?

The Treaty of Guadalupe Hidalgo between Mexico and the U.S. ensured that marriages recognized as legal in Mexico be recognized in the U.S. In addition, few Mexican men, whether rich or poor, married white women, who were in short supply. In contrast, many white men married Mexican women, especially those of significant wealth. According to Horace Bell, it was largely Mexican daughters of well-off families who married good-looking but lazy vagabond Americans whose object of marriage seems to have been to get rich without having to work. Many of these women were brought to ruin as a result (1930). According to Jayne Dysart, marrying white men was recognized by Mexican families who found themselves living in the U.S. as a means to protect their landholdings. Dysart notes that in San Antonio between 1837 and 1860, one daughter from almost every Mexican family holding land married a white American man.[71]

The inclusion of Mexicans within whiteness for the purposed of marriage served the economic interests of white men. The exclusion of Mexicans from whiteness for the purpose of testifying against whites, the assignment of wages and conditions of labor, and the many other civil, political and social rights of citizenship, were believed to serve the same interests. I say "believed" because it is possible, if not probable, that had laborers not allowed themselves to be divided or participated in the divisions among themselves (white, not white, male, female, etc...), they would have held more strength in unity when seeking improved conditions and wages.

The experience of Mexicans in the United States reveals the limits of inclusion within the category white conferred by law, without the pervasive constructive and enforcement efforts such as we saw in law following Bacon's Rebellion (at least, when the status as white is contested). Being white by federal law was not without its advantages, including the ability to naturalize. It also resulted in few restrictions on marital relations, though it is certainly possible that this would have been otherwise had these marriages not served the interests of white men so well. Being white by federal law failed to secure much else, and did little to advance the social acceptance of Mexicans as white. If the standard of measure from the colonial era of being sufficiently like the British continued, Mexicans were determined to be insufficiently so.

Naturalization was an area of law that worked to advance America as white. The value of being white within the U.S. was recognized internationally and reflected in the treaties the U.S. negotiated with Mexico and Spain. Rather than secure whiteness for Mexicans, this worked to render them white for purposes of some laws (specifically, antimiscegenation and naturalization), but not "really" white. As a result, Mexicans at this time were rendered "contingent whites." Contingent, because their status depends upon the legal imposition of the label "white" and has little meaning for them outside of those areas of federal law that require the status white for the benefits the law secures. While Mexicans in North America may have been the first in this racial location, they certainly have not been the last.[72]

It is helpful to consider T.S. Marshall's three components of citizenship rights – civil, political, and social – in order to best capture the experience of Mexicans in the U.S. relative to full citizenship (1964). The civil rights component consists of those rights that enable individual freedom, and include the right to contract and to own property and the right to justice. These rights were not protected for Mexican people. Political rights of citizenship consist of the right to engage in the political process as a member or an elector of those who make up that representative body. This was perhaps the right of citizenship rendered most available, but was often threatened by Nativist activity. Social rights of citizenship were very limited for Mexicans, and consist of such things as a measure of economic welfare and security, to the right to fully participate in the social heritage, and to a civilized life as measured by the prevailing social standards. It is worth noting again that social rights of citizenship are required for the exercise of both civil and political rights. In other words, adequate economic and basic social resources including security are necessary in order to be able to vote or run for office or to experience individual freedom. Marshall's full citizenship helps to identify how narrow the experience of citizenship was made for Mexicans in the U.S.[73]

The experience of Mexicans and Mexican-Americans in the U.S. following the Treaty of Guadalupe-Hidalgo reveals a democratization in the determination of who is white. This can be seen not only in the example of persons of Mexican descent but in the experience of the Irish and other immigrants who came in large numbers and faced tremendous resistance to their full inclusion in America. Full inclusion in the new republic required being viewed as white.

From Green to White

The Irish Catholics, who came in large numbers to U.S. shores during the nineteenth century, help to make visible the ways in which race shaped the society within which they sought, enacted, and eventually won status as white. Before 1830, most white immigrants to the U.S were Protestants from England or other parts of Europe. Historian Kirby Miller notes that the Irish who came from 1815 through 1844 numbered between 800,000 and one million and reflected characteristics and qualities of many other immigrants to America during this period; the majority were not Catholic and they were not all poor (1985). In contrast, the 1.8 million Irish who came in the ten-year span between 1845 and 1855, many fleeing starvation in Ireland, were generally poorer than earlier arrivals to the U.S. and were largely Catholic. Between 43 percent and 47 percent of immigrants each year from 1820 to 1855 came from Ireland.[74]

Large numbers of poor Irish lived in "trinity" houses, small alley houses erected between large streets, that were three stories high with one room on each floor, or in small lodging-houses in very difficult conditions where hunger, filth and poor health flourished. An 1853 report on living conditions in a heavily Irish district in Philadelphia provides the following description:

> We will essay a description of a hovel we visited.... It is a two-story frame of quite a small size, but is nevertheless divided into a number of rooms which are about ten feet square. The bar room is in front on the ground floor. With

the exception of this apartment, no other part of the house contained a single article of furniture, except some damaged furnaces and miserable stoves. The walls were discolored by smoke and filth, the glass was broken from the windows, chinks in the frame work let in the cold air, and every thing was as wretchedly uncomfortable as it is possible to conceive. Yet in every one of these squalid apartments, including the cellar and the loft, men and women – blacks and whites by dozens – were huddled together promiscuously, squatting or lying upon bare floors, and keeping themselves from freezing by covering their bodies with such filthy rags as chance threw in their way.

The conditions they faced were particularly harsh in part because the famine Irish entered the U.S. workforce at the very bottom, competing only with free people of African descent in the north and, in the south, with slave labor. Upon arrival in the U.S., Irish Catholics were often lumped together with persons of African descent both at work and in neighborhoods.[75]

At the time when large numbers of Irish Catholics arrived, the U.S. was itself increasingly divided between those invested in slavery and those who opposed its spread to the territories. Because such large numbers of Irish arrived in such a short period of time and because they were largely centralized in cities in the north, they became a significant political contingency that would impact the national debate. Where their allegiances would fall was by no means a foregone conclusion. It is in the struggle over the Irish and of the Irish that the constraints and possibilities within their adopted homeland become apparent, and that whiteness is revealed as central.

Irish Catholics in the U.S. were portrayed as anti-American, not full citizens, and as "white negroes." These portrayals came largely from nativist segments of the Whig party. In sharp contrast, the Irish were claimed as fellow whites by Democrats and portrayed as victims of "wage slavery." Before proceeding with the experience of the Irish in the U.S., it is helpful to note something of the national political landscape that significantly shaped their experience, as these portrayals suggest.

Political Landscape

American political party rivalries following the signing of the Constitution were represented by the Federalists and the Republicans. As the Federalists became increasingly pro-British and regional in the northeast, they faded after the War of 1812. The result was that Republicans enjoyed a decade of largely unchallenged dominance. It would be incorrect to view this period of a single party as one of national solidarity, however. Factionalism was present and building before it finally "erupted into rebellion against the last Republican administration, that of John Quincy Adams. Andrew Jackson's victory over Adams in 1828 led to a renewal of overt party competition..." Jacksonians transformed into the *Democratic* Party. The supporters of Adams were *Republican, National Republican,* and eventually, *Whig.* These shifts reflected the struggle to create a sustainable coalition.[76]

The merchant-landlord coalition was the base of the Republican Party, and likewise was the base of the Whig party when it emerged. This coalition was rendered difficult by more diversified economic growth since 1812, creating new fractures and challenges. These were only exacerbated by the crisis of 1819-1820, over whether Missouri would be admitted to the union as a free or slave state, and exposed a regional split in the coalition that led to the collapse of Jefferson's party. At the same time, the crisis revealed to slaveholders the need for a new party to secure their interests within the Union. The man who would build this party was Martin Van Buren, and the Democratic Party was the party he built. Before examining the Democratic Party, I will discuss its primary opponent – the Whigs.

Whigs believed that power properly followed wealth, and therefore believed that those of the upper class were the only responsible men who could administer a republican form of government. Central to their idea of responsible government was a social order that was constituted by ownership of property. They emphasized education and moral sensibility derived from upper-class culture as critical to a nation, especially a new one. The Whigs consisted of a coalition of regional elites who were held together in their value of upper-class refinements and support of national development. However, the Whig party evaporated in the south as the interests of slave-based commercial agriculture diverged from those of the merchant-landlord.[77]

The Democratic Party that Van Buren built through the instrument of the man who would be the seventh president of the U.S., Andrew Jackson, succeeded in continuous Democratic rule from 1828-1860. It was the first party based upon popular constituencies, and enacted electoral reforms (removing the requirement of property ownership as a prerequisite to vote) resulting in the most democratic republic of its time and perhaps ever since. The Democratic Party combined the planters of the south and plain Republicans who were largely laborers and artisans of the north. What could hold these seemingly disparate groups together? What interests did they share?

The planters of the south, of course, were invested in the preservation of slavery. The workers of the north, a significant portion of who were Irish, were interested in the preservation of life and limb through the sale of their labor. They sought to defend their claims to citizenship, in part, through access to naturalization. Both were under attack by nativists. The Democratic Party appealed to immigrant laborers of the north, including the Irish, in part because the party rejected nativism. According the Ignatiev, "the need to gain the loyalty of the Irish explains why the Democratic Party, on the whole, rejected nativism." Some southern planters and those loyal to them spoke against "wage slavery," earning them the gratitude of some northern workers for exposing the conditions under which they labor. The Democratic Party also offered something all-American for the Irish to utilize and claim – white supremacy. "White unity," promulgated by the Democratic Party, helped to silence questions about the qualifications of the Irish for citizenship, because their allegiance to the party asserted the Irish as white.[78]

The polarized national political landscape, with Whigs and their strong nativist tendencies on the one hand, and Democrats who advocated white supremacy above all on the other, helps to capture the pressures and possibilities presented the Irish who ventured to American shores. This alone, however, does not capture the complete picture, because politics, labor, and virtually every other aspect of life was played out within a social environment that was thoroughly racialized. What this means is that everyone in the U.S. was assigned a place on a race spectrum on which whites and blacks represented polar opposites.

The Racial Landscape

Black people had so thoroughly been defined as anathema to citizenship and as the direct opposite of that which was valued in America (i.e., freedom), while white people represented full citizenship and freedom and were presumed superior to all groups constructed as other-than-white. Regardless of an individual's education, skill, or qualities, racial categories were rendered pre-eminent in the award or denial of resources, opportunities, and social acceptance as a "full citizen" or "real American."

As a result, the surest route to success in America was in and through whiteness. This, of course, presented a challenge to a group who lived and worked within such close proximity to black people. Many Irish Catholics desperate for work faced treacherous conditions that placed them in regular contact with black laborers, and that sometimes placed them as less valuable than slave labor. Most Irish men worked at some point as canal, railroad, construction, or dock laborers, while Irish women often worked as domestic servants.

Sometimes Irish workers were preferred over black slaves because the latter had a higher economic value. An Alabama company official explaining "why Irish workers were employed on the docks: 'The niggers are worth too much to be risked here; if the Paddies are knocked over-board, or get their backs broke, nobody loses anything.' When the commissioner of the (New Orleans) New Basin Canal Corporation began building in 1831, they knew that the mortality rate among the laborers would be high; consequently they hired Irish." Irish in the U.S. were disproportionately laborers and servants. Many entered the labor force doing work that was relegated only to those of African descent, and offered to perform the work at wages below that which African Americans were previously hired. These conditions of labor rendered the Irish vulnerable to being linked with the wrong end of the racial hierarchy in the U.S., and helps explain the label "white negroes."[79]

How is one's whiteness established in such a context? Since the founding of the U.S., white people included only those who performed "white man's work." According to Ignatiev, "It was not enough for the Irish to have a competitive advantage over Afro-Americans in the labor market; in order for them to avoid a taint of blackness it was necessary that no Negro be allowed to work in occupations where Irish were to be found." Through the use and refusal of their labor, the Irish succeeded in taking the lowest of jobs and squeezing those of African descent out. This was accomplished by the refusal of white laborers to work with a black laborer. The *African Repository* reported in 1851:

> In New York and other eastern cities, the influx of white laborers has expelled the Negro almost en masse from the exercise of the ordinary branches of labor. You no longer see him work upon buildings, and rarely is he allowed to drive a cart of public conveyance. White men will not work with him.[80]

Through their refusal to work with black laborers, the Irish not only advanced their labor interests but worked to establish themselves as white.

Many native-born artisans linked unfavorable changes in their conditions of work and wages with the arrival of the Irish Catholics, and expressed this frustration and location of blame through anti-immigrant riots and anti-immigrant political movements (i.e., nativism). For the masses of Irish Catholics who lived and labored under conditions of incredible hardship, there were few resources to drawn upon in order to contest such assaults, other than that provided by their sheer numbers. It was not numbers alone, however, that gave power to the Irish. There were two critical factors: first was access to naturalization and therefore citizenship; the second was a racialized social context. Access to citizenship combined with the tendency of the Irish to amass in larger cities resulted in their becoming a political force in elections. In fact, by 1844 the Irish constituted the most impervious voting block in the country with the sole exception of free blacks, whose votes were cast in the opposite direction than those of the Irish. The racial landscape upon which all in the U.S. were required to navigate not only presented challenges, but opportunities. David

Roediger explains that by "casting job competition and neighborhood rivalries as racial," rather than ethnic or religious, the Irish repeatedly asserted themselves as white people and pushed back against the nativist logic that portrayed foreign-born citizens as un-American, not "full citizens."[81]

It is therefore not surprising that the Irish focused their labor competition upon free blacks in the north and upon Chinese on the west coast, rather than upon other groups. The racial landscape assisted them in this focus, since persons of African and Chinese descent in the U.S. were much less able to strike back. Therefore, they could more easily be marginalized and excluded, hated and harmed. Here, the racial landscape provided resources that could be exploited for the benefit of Irish in North America.

Black people were rendered more and more marginal to the assets and opportunities of America through exclusion, labor exploitation, and disenfranchisement at the very time when the vote was being advanced for white men during the Jacksonian period (1824-1848). Irish Catholic immigrants quickly learned that persons of African descent (and later the Chinese) in the U.S. could be hated and harmed with impunity. "If the Constitution did not formally guarantee to whites the right to engage in mob attacks on black people, that right was safeguarded in the Jacksonian age by the absence of anything like a modern state. The city relied on volunteers to defend public order." While the Irish and all other immigrants of this period learned that black people in America represented the opposite of free, they also learned that the best way to defend jobs and claim rights in the U.S. was "as 'white' entitlements."[82]

Many have asked why the competition among Irish- and Afro-American laborers failed to lead to recognition of the need for unity. During Bacon's Rebellion in 1678, laborers of British and African descent united against the landowning elite. Why not the Irish and free blacks in the 1840s? The answer, of course, is that competition between these two groups did not take place under normal circumstances of labor conflict.[83] Instead, it took place upon a playing field of white people and non-white people that gave unearned advantages to those seen as white and unearned disadvantages to those understood as not white. Upon this playing field, those seen as white people, those viewed as fit for citizenship via naturalization, were being pressured by nativist sentiment to exclude large groups of recent arrivals, including the Irish.

The racial social context within which Irish competed for work can be seen most vividly in efforts to exclude by virtue of race. Arguably, the greatest competition to Irish labor came from other Irish immigrants, and then German immigrants, more than free blacks. The Irish quickly learned that race, specifically whiteness, was key to success in work and politics. For example, Irish dockworkers in New York tried to expel German longshoremen by claiming that they sought an all-white work force. As we know, they were not successful in labeling the Germans as other-than-white. There was, however, no contestation to the claim that persons of African descent were not white. Free blacks in the north and Chinese on the west coast *could* be marginalized. Their exclusion from whiteness opened that door. As a result, German immigrants rather than free blacks were more successful competitors over jobs, since they had access to citizenship as whites, could therefore seek to voice their interests at elections, and could claim both jobs and rights as white entitlements.[84]

The Call to Abolition

It was within this national political environment and racialized context in the U.S. that some 60,000 Irish issued an address in 1841 to their compatriots in North America, imploring them to join with the abolitionists and oppose slavery upon the new soil they called home. Ireland had a long and violent past with invaders, namely the British, who sought to displace, control, and exploit its native people and natural resources. This experience shaped Ireland's strong and early opposition to slavery. The tide of opposition to slavery out of Ireland, however, was short-lived and was likely connected to the charisma of Daniel O'Connel, a signatory to the address, who came to the U.S. to encourage support.[85]

Response to the address was strong and immediate. A meeting of Irish miners in Pottsville, Pennsylvania put into question the authenticity of the address. The miners referenced themselves as *full citizens* of the U.S. and declared that they were not willing to look upon black Africans as their "brethren." They noted that slavery was a legacy of British rule and argued that those abroad had no business critiquing or seeking to influence matters of national policy.[86]

Arguably the most influential leader of Irish in America was the Catholic Bishop of New York, John J. Hughs. The Bishop responded to the address by questioning its authenticity and claiming that it was:

> The duty of every naturalized Irishman to resist and repudiate the address with indignation. Not precisely because of the doctrines it contains, but because of their having emanated from a foreign source, and of their tendency to operate on questions of domestic and national policy. I am no friend of slavery, but I am still less friendly to any attempt of foreign origin to abolish.
>
> The duty of naturalized Irishmen or others, I consider to be in no wise distinct or different from those of native born Americans....[87]

At a meeting to address Irish Repeal and American Slavery held on November 18, 1843, in Philadelphia, a Mr. O'Brien stated that he personally was opposed to slavery but saw it as his duty to uphold American institutions, of which slavery is a significant and foundational one.[88]

These responses by Irish in America to the address were the norm. They are best understood within the context of strong nativism and a racial landscape that permeated every aspect of society. Within the framework of naturalization law, the only access to citizenship for those born outside the U.S (and therefore not native to it), the claim of the miners that they are "full citizens" was simultaneously an assertion of a status as white. As we know, naturalization was rendered a white-only process. So for those not native born, claims to citizenship were simultaneously claims to whiteness, and claims to whiteness were simultaneously claims to being American.

The replies to the address must also be understood, in part, as a response to the strong nativist arguments that foreign-born U.S. citizens do not represent the best interests of America but are influenced instead by foreign concerns. For example, after the 1844 presidential election that placed Polk in the White House, the Whig politician John Pendleton Kennedy attributed the Whig candidate's (Henry Clay) defeat to the foreign vote in a letter to the New York *Tribune*. Kennedy claimed that the voice of the true people of America was being outweighed by those un-Americans who do not know the difference between American and foreign interests.[89]

In the face of accusations by native-born Americans that the sentiment of the Irish expressed at the ballot box in America is motivated by the best interests of Ireland, the responses to the address are not surprising. Bishop Hughs and the Pottsville miners rejected any appearance of foreign influence upon the Irish in America. The two areas wherein the Irish were most vulnerable to accusations of outside influence were both addressed by man at the Irish Repeal and American Slavery meeting in Philadelphia. He identified himself as vice-president of the Repeal Association in Boston and stated, to repeated cheers, that even if O'Connell (representing Ireland) and the Pope (representing Catholicism) were abolitionists, neither spoke for the Irish in the America.[90]

Nativism in the Whig party and the racial landscape in the U.S. made it less likely that the Irish would recall their own struggles against slavery and exploitation by the British and join the abolitionist movement. The nativism of the Whigs all but determined that the newly arrived Irish would find refuge in the Democratic Party. As it turned out, they found much more. The party of white supremacy served up a resource that assisted the Irish in becoming white in America.

As we saw in chapters one and two, when white people were first invented and asserted as a group of humanity in the decades after Bacon's Rebellion, the invention functioned to divide laborers and unite whites. Here again, some one hundred and fifty years later, we see that the invention of white people served to divide those whose social position was most similar – Irish Catholics and free blacks – and unite those who shared far less: Irish Catholics and white Protestant slaveholders. The historical results are profound. Assimilation of the Irish into the white race allowed slavery to continue for at least fifteen years while the existence of a racialized society, consisting most generally of whites and nonwhites, allowed for that assimilation.

The pressures that nativism imposed and the "playing field" that racial constructs in the U.S. presented significantly shaped that which was possible for Irish Catholics in North America. However, the paths taken were not the only possibilities. The period in American history when so many downtrodden outsiders arrived upon her shores represents one of those moments when significant alteration from the status quo was possible. Enough pieces were present, including a people with a history of exploitation and enslavement who were outsiders upon arrival in Protestant America, and who constituted enough of a concentrated constituency to make an impact.

The experience of Mexicans in the U.S. after the Mexican-American War and that of Irish Catholics reveals not only the value that being white had come to represent, but the struggle to control the determination of those who were "really" white. We see through these groups that Mexicans were excluded from whiteness at the local level despite federal law, and that Irish were included through the exercise of white supremacy at the local level and by virtue of political allegiance. Becoming "really" white was fought out in the muddy waters of labor competition between and among laborers – the divisive purpose for the invention of white people in the first place. As such, history can only evaluate white people as a huge success.

Discussion Questions:

1. What factors likely played a role in the exclusion of Mexicans from being included as white for the purpose of everyday interactions?
2. What factors likely played a role in Mexicans counting as white for the purpose of antimiscegenation law?
3. When you consider the experience of Mexicans in the U.S. after the Treaty of Guadalupe Hidalgo and compare it to that of the Irish Catholics, what factors worked to the advantage of the Irish?
4. What forces and pressures helped influence the masses of Irish Catholics to take an anti-abolition stance rather than support the abolition of slavery?

CHAPTER 5

Seeing White and Naming Injustice

From the moment that white people were invented, the category has been integrally tied with the control of women and nonwhite men and the interests of the wealthiest capitalists. While white people are clearly a fiction, the organization of society and relationships that the fiction structured are very real and have resulted in consequences that have provided white people material and symbolic resources throughout U.S. history. How might a social construct with these roots be challenged?

The term "whiteness" captures the fictions integral to and realities resulting from the social construct called white people. In other words, whiteness captures not only those people labeled as white but, more significantly, the dominant ideas about them that sustain the group and the organization of society that these ideas have shaped. The histories within chapters one through four reveal whiteness to be divisive and an abrogation of the promise of liberty, justice and equal opportunity in the United States. The histories, first and foremost, expose that the "white race" is a product of human action rather than nature. As a result, the histories redirect our focus away from racial explanations and instead point toward social structural explanations for social phenomena, patterns, and individual experience. Both of these will be discussed in detail, and their significance for the dismantling of whiteness considered.

The invention of white people has had a lasting impact, not the least of which is the persistence of the belief that white people constitute a unique group of humanity – a race. The history of the invention of white people exposes the "white race" for what it is: a historical creation to serve the interests of the wealthiest capitalists and provide unearned advantages for those labeled white, and unearned disadvantages to those labeled other-than-white. The invention has served the interests of the wealthiest by keeping laborers divided, viewing each other as competition along so-called race lines rather than collective strength as was demonstrated in Bacon's Rebellion.

The invention of white people has worked not only to divide laborers from each other, but has caused white laborers to perceive a stronger link with those whose social condition and class is dramatically different from their own, on the sole basis of sharing a fictitious race. White people do share something as white people, but it is nothing biologically-based, nothing racial; it is social and the result of common advantages that have generated shared experiences, perceptions, and expectations. These combine to constitute white culture. There is a tremendous range of advantage among white people depending upon any number of significant social factors, such as class, religion, abilities, and gender, among others. This fact, however, does not erase that all whites share to some degree in the overall package of advantages conferred upon them at any given historical moment on the basis of their being viewed as white.

For example, even the poorest British bond-laborers, following the post-Bacon's Rebellion enactments asserting white people, experienced privilege by virtue of having been made white. Law demanded it. It did not matter whether any individual wanted such privileges or not. Privileges on the basis of whiteness were conferred via the very organization of society from basic human interactions, including prohibitions on intermingling and miscegenation, to the structure of work wherein whites were placed in positions of management over nonwhites, to the ability to survive and defend one's self and one's family with laws that required white men to receive a gun and powder upon completion of their term of bond-labor and denied gun possession by law to persons of African descent.

The history examined in chapters one through four reveals the existence of the group called white people and the belief in their supremacy as inseparable. Superiority is the logic or the glue for the grouping. This is not to say that members of the group are in fact superior intellectually, physically or otherwise, but rather, that superiority served as the reason to justify the creation of the group. This was true in 1681, when "white" first appeared in law and assumed ideas about the British as those deserving of rights and privileges from which others can be denied. It was true in 1790 when Congress rendered naturalization a white-only process. It has been true ever since in labor struggles that have manifested as whites claiming "their" jobs as Americans. It manifests in many ways in contemporary U.S. society, some of which are explored in the afterword of this book. Because white people were a creation of people, not nature, the demise of this invention demands a fracturing of the very idea of the white race and its superiority.

Being aware of the history of the invention of white people is important because that awareness helps to contest the commonly held belief that whites are a distinct group of humanity united by biology or genetics. This alone is powerful, because it directs one to different questions and actions. When patterns arise that are linked to people grouped as white or not white, such as that of white people having higher rates of upward mobility (for example), the awareness moves us away from racial or essentialist explanations – for example, that white people are more successful because they are more intelligent – and begs the question, "What social forces and what historical practices might help explain the pattern of higher levels of financial success among those labeled white in the past and today?" The shift from thinking about groups of people possessing qualities by virtue of the group (i.e., white, black, Asian, tribal member, etc…) to thinking about the structures put in place as a result of the invented groups and meanings attached is key.

The histories in the preceding chapters reveal that one of the greatest roadblocks to the promise of equal opportunity is the institutionalization of the idea of white people as a biological reality reflecting a superior group of humanity. If equal opportunity, liberty and justice for all are ideals to which we strive, then these beliefs and the structures they sustain must be dismantled. They begin to be fractured by awareness of the social construction of race, including the white race. Awareness invites new ways of being and acting because common practices that rely upon the belief in white people as a product of nature no longer hold the power they once did.

Jacqueline Battalora

Hard Work and the American Dream

Most children in the United States grow up learning that America is a land of equal opportunity offering liberty and justice for all. The message, we are told, is that if you work hard, you will eventually succeed. Success is generally defined as having a spouse, two children, and a dog, owning a car or two and a home with a white picket fence, and having a financial nest for eventual retirement. It is hard to escape childhood without being indoctrinated in this American ideology. This ideology, however, is simply untrue, and even harmful.

The history of the invention of white people and the institutionalization of whiteness in the U.S. among so much American history requires that this ideology be reassessed. The histories examined in chapters one through four reveal that inequality has been foundational as a matter of law in the U.S. To be more precise, the presumed superiority of white people was institutionalized within law and policy from the very founding of the country, and has awarded whites unearned advantages.

The American ideology of hard work and success is not only problematic because it is not sustained by facts; it is also harmful. Children are told from their earliest years that everyone can succeed in America if you work hard. This message fails to account for the dramatically unequal playing field upon which people work to succeed. The message erases the many structural advantages that white people (men in particular) have been afforded, from access to citizenship, higher wages, better jobs, access to advancement, cheaper property, and less competition in every area of society, including access to women and the institution of marriage.

The message of this American ideology erases the many structural hurdles that those rendered not white, including persons of African descent, members of native tribes, Chinese, Japanese, and Mexicans, to name a few, have had to confront as they work hard to succeed. These structural hurdles have certainly restricted and in some cases blocked success, even when one engaged regularly in hard work. Here is where the ideology is particularly harmful. The message of the ideology is that if you do not succeed, if you do not accomplish the American dream, it is your fault. The message is that any failure to accomplish the dream is the result of *personal* failure. You simply did not work hard enough. The structural roadblocks that exclusion from whiteness have presented, from denial of citizenship to the lowest of wages, and exclusion from neighborhoods, jobs, education, and opportunities, are all erased in a single ideological claim.

Conversely, when white people realize the American dream, credit is given as if there were no unearned advantage along the way. This is not to say that white people have not faced incredibly difficult situations and had to work very hard. Irish Catholics in the mid-nineteenth century are one among many examples of people who faced incredible hardship and worked very hard to improve their lot. It is simply undeniable that their status as white in the U.S. afforded them opportunities and access denied to those rendered not white. Without being successful in asserting themselves as white, Irish Catholics would have found themselves along a path much more similar to the Chinese and free persons of African descent in the U.S. It was only through the assertion of the Irish as white that they gained full citizenship and became a force on election days.

Having equal opportunity, liberty, and justice for all as *goals* that this country strives to achieve is admirable, and can serve the country well in guiding policies and action. It is important that these ideals not be portrayed as realized, and it is important that hard work be valued without erasing social structural realities that give a greater reward, including recognition for the hard work of some over others. Equal opportunity, liberty, and justice must be held out as principles that, to date, the country has afforded in different degrees to different groups at different times, and must strive to offer all.

If the United States is going to take steps toward the ideals it espouses, we must be honest; we must assess and plan relying upon facts, not fiction. I can think of no greater fiction embedded within the fabric of this country's founding law and policies than the existence of a separate and distinct group of humanity called the "white race."

Jacqueline Battalora

Dismantling One of the World's Most Harmful Constructs

Because whiteness as a facet of reality and object of knowledge is not necessary by nature, it must be constantly maintained and re-affirmed in order to persist. Indeed, a social construct like white people and the idea of various human "races" that it helps maintain requires a dynamic process of production, re-production, and institutionalization to be rendered common knowledge. The imposition of the human category white was originally imposed by elite lawmakers, but was soon enacted by white laborers. The degree of investment in whiteness on the part of laborers can be seen in the efforts of native-born Americans to exclude Chinese laborers and Mexicans in order to advance their own interests on the *basis* of whiteness and, with regard to the latter, on the basis of being "really" white. It can be seen in the struggle of Irish Catholics in the mid-nineteenth century to gain acceptance and a footing in America *through* a claim to whiteness.

Because whiteness begins to be fractured by the very recognition of its fictitiousness as a race, widespread recognition of white people as a social construct can dramatically transform society. This is true because the awareness demands a new focus. As previously noted, the awareness results in a shift from "race" to the social conditions that such an invention has made. The dominant construction of race however, presents a challenge. Let me explain.

When a television show is "about race," who constitutes the topic of the show? Do white people? When a course or seminar is concerned with race, who is being read or discussed? Is it white people? Most of the time, such media presentations or instructional content address nonwhite people. Because of this practice, in part, the word race has come to connote nonwhites. The perceptual trickery of this conception of race is that whiteness escapes any sort of connection to the organization of groups of people called "racial" groups. As a result, experience derived from the status white is not seen as a result of that racial status. The racialness of whiteness is rendered invisible. It is simply – what is.

Talking about race here is tricky. The histories and analysis deployed in this book expose whites as a biological reality to be fictitious. In so doing, they expose the concept of "race" as reflecting distinct groups of humanity to also be a fiction. So as we proceed and the word "race" is utilized, it is drawn upon in the same way that "white" has been utilized – to reflect the lived reality that the fiction created. In other words, because so much of life has been organized around the belief, however false, that blacks and whites, for example, constitute separate and distinct groups of people, I use the word "race" to reflect this lived reality that the construct of race has engendered.

The erasure of race from whiteness is a post-civil rights era phenomenon. Prior to the 1950s, there was little resistance on a mass scale to the view that the white race was superior. This view was challenged during the civil rights movement. The racial organization of U.S. society was transformed by the civil rights movement, and so too was whiteness. The white race became the unspoken norm rather than an explicitly expressed racial location from which laws and policies are advocated. One result is that experience derived from the point of view of white people is treated today as simply "the truth" rather than a partial truth contained by a racial status among other factors including gender, class, religion, abilities, etc.

For instance, the view of a historical moment passed to us through the writings of a white male, like Thomas Jefferson, is often given a universal truth status. His words and perceptions are not viewed as shaped by his experiences in society as a white person. Contrast that with a historical figure who shares the same gender status but is not white, like Frederick Douglass, whose writings are not seen as the truth for all people. Rather, his ideas and claims are viewed as shaped by his African ancestry, his blackness. His ideas, unlike those of a white person, are seen as coming from the specific racial perspective of a black man in the U.S. In contrast, the ideas and proclamations of Thomas Jefferson reflect the perspective of a reformer, a revolutionary. His ideas and words are not viewed as racially contained and shaped. Therefore, the white racial perspective that shaped Jefferson's ideas and proclamations is generally missing from consideration. Being black certainly shaped Frederick Douglass' ideas and perceptions. Being white shaped Thomas Jefferson's.

While race is no more a biological reality than white people, the realities that race has shaped within society demand that we examine white people within the context of the larger racial framework: as a social status given tremendous meaning. Failure to do so blocks a complete picture of the social structural impact of being classified within the group called white. The tendency to miss the "racialness" of white experience has numerous effects. First, it fails to capture the significant impact that a white racial status has upon one's life experience and one's perceptions. Second, it keeps the social structural consequences of a white racial status invisible. In addition, it is a reaffirming practice because the tendency to miss the racial dimensions of whiteness works to render a white racial status invisible.

A result of the dominant conception of race, a conception that misses white people as a part of the larger racial fabric, is that white people get away with advocating for certain things such as policies, legislation, practices, and so forth as if they are race-neutral. The truth is a white person is no more race-neutral than a Hispanic, Chinese, Japanese, African American or any other person. The difference is that the latter are *seen* as racial beings, and white people are not.

Whiteness has been sustained for more than three hundred years in the U.S. because it is continuously reinforced and re-enacted. In its current form whiteness is not even seen, because it has been stripped from dominant conceptions of race. Knowing that white people are a biological fiction constitutes a critical step toward the dismantling of race and institutionalized white supremacy in the United States. Another critical step is for the whiteness within our structures of thought and social organizations to be identified and named.

When whiteness is seen as a social construct with real consequences that must be identified *as white* within the larger framework of fabricated races, we can examine almost any law, policy, ideology or practice and begin to consider the presence and workings of whiteness. An example of this sort of examination was conducted above in our consideration of American ideology regarding hard work and the American dream. For those who want to engage in the work of dismantling institutionalized white supremacy, this is one of the most demanding projects before you – seeing whiteness and naming it. You already hold the most important piece of knowledge – that white people and claims of their superiority constitute this country's greatest work of fiction.

Afterword:
Why Would Whites Work to Dismantle Whiteness?

People often ask me why white people would challenge whiteness, since it confers so many unearned advantages to those classified as or merely presumed to be white. There are a number of motivating factors. First, when white people become aware of their unearned advantages and understand that such advantages only exist by virtue of unearned harms meted out to those race-ed other than white, most are unnerved by the injustice. Additionally, as whites realize that the preferential meanings that have been assigned to the status white only exist by virtue of the degradation of those rendered not white or contingent white, for no other reason than their "racial" status, they are interested in correcting this social inequality.

It may seem counterintuitive for someone who enjoys the material and symbolic value of being labeled white to be invested in dismantling whiteness. However, material and symbolic value are not the only consequences of whiteness. Even if a person labeled white is not interested in the national project of taking steps in the direction of the country's ideals, there are other reasons for white people to be invested in the project of dismantling whiteness.

I have lived in Chicago as an adult since the 1990s. During this decade and since, gang violence is regularly portrayed on the evening news. Hearing of a bystander, often a young child, shot by stray bullets at the hands of a gang member has been far too common. I recall hearing colleagues, friends and strangers comment on these members as somehow defective, suffering from a loss of humanity, having lost any sense of the value of life.

When learning about the atrocities inflicted upon Jewish people by Nazis during World War Two, I remember asking, "How could the German soldiers and the many others who participated do such things to another human being?" The presumption, of course, is that engaging in acts and omissions that exhibit such disregard for another human being reflects a defect. Specifically, this question points to a defect in one's humanity.

In my efforts to understand the ways in which whiteness has been enacted and imposed, historical records have proven vital. This history aids in understanding what whiteness is, from where it has come, and the purposes it serves. This history is no less important in identifying the harm of white supremacy than it is in examining the privilege that institutionalized white supremacy confers. There is a particularly disturbing area of U.S. history that provides the most dramatic and clear display of the harm to white people that is a direct result of white supremacy. That history is of lynching.

A lynching is an extra-judicial killing of a person, usually by a group of people often referred to as a mob. A small slice of the history of lynching in the U.S. is being drawn upon, not to promote guilt or agitate hatred. Rather, the history of lynching is important in order to help ensure that such atrocities are not repeated again, and for our purposes the history of lynching helps expose the harm to white people's humanity that white supremacy has inflicted. The images we will examine are important not only because they capture through the lens of a camera brutal violence inflicted without judge, jury, or any due process of law, but also because they expose a deeply deficient humanity.

An African American was vulnerable to a white lynch mob whenever he or she was accused, whether substantiated or not, of violating white supremacy. In the record of lynching that follows, these include being accused of striking a white police officer, being accused of stealing from a white person, being accused of assaulting a white woman, or simply being unfortunate enough to be in the company of an African American so accused when the mob arrived.

Photograph number one is from the day Rubin Stacy was lynched in July 1935, in Florida. Look at how the people who stand behind the hanging body of Rubin Stacy are dressed. What does their dress suggest? Look at how they are standing. What do their gestures and positioning/ posturing say about their thoughts or feelings in the moment? Look at the young girl on the left with a big smile on her face. Look at the other even younger girls to the right of Rubin's hanging corps. Pay attention to the faces of those who are witnessing this murder, or at least its aftermath. What do you see? What would you expect to see in the face of one who retained her or his full humanity? What do you think these young white girls are learning from the lynching exhibition?

Photograph number two that follows is from the murder of Lige Daniels in August 1920 in Texas. Unlike Florida, this image reveals only males within the frame of the image, both boys and men. There are both stern looks and smiles on the faces of the crowd of males who stand beneath the hanging corpse of Mr. Daniels. Again, young children appear in the image. The young man in the center of the image wearing a tie is also wearing a big smile. Look at how many men and boys gathered for the lynching or its aftermath. Those in the image appear to be posing for the photograph that includes the hanging corpse of Lige Daniels.

Photograph number three is striking because it captures a wide-angle view of a lynch scene from November 1909 in Cairo, Illinois. Look at the numbers of people who came to participate in the spectacle. What does it say about how white participants responded to lynching? Does this images suggest a celebration, mourning, disgust, joy, excitement?

Photograph number four is of the charred body of Jessie Washington from 1916 in Waco, Texas. Look at the faces of the white participants. Do these faces reveal disgust and horror? How would you expect a person who exemplifies the capacities of human dignity to respond to the burning of a human being? The charred body of Jessie Washington was photographed, made into souvenir postcards and sold for ten cents. Notice in the foreground the tops of the heads of small children right in front of Jesse Washington's corps.[91]

Photograph number five is from the murder of Abram Smith and Thomas Shipp in August 1930 at the hands of a white lynch mob in Marion, Indiana captures again the sheer numbers of whites who were drawn to a lynching. It also suggests how such violence asserted by whites was received by the larger community of whites who came out to participate. Look in the foreground on the left side of the image and

Photograph 1

Photograph 2

Photograph 3

Photograph 4

Photograph 5

you will see a young couple who appear to be on a date. If the image were expanded you would see that they are holding hands. Just to the right of them is a woman with shoulder length dark hair. Again, if the image were expanded you would see that she appears to be in the last trimester of pregnancy. Look at the smiles and laughter that appear on many of the faces of those who stand near the bloodied hanging bodies of two men.

The harm from white supremacy that these lynching images capture is not only the blatant murderous harm to those communities who were the target of white lynch mobs. These images reveal a defective humanity within those communities that enacted and participated in lynching, and within a nation that condoned lynching by failing to prosecute those who murdered. The history of lynching reveals harm and the effects of brutal violence at multiple levels. It dramatically exposes the harm to black Americans whose bodies were tortured, hung, burned and dismembered. Just as there is general recognition that something was wrong with those German soldiers who participated in the slaughter of other humans labeled Jews, gays, or disabled people, there is evidence of a similar defect in the white people who participated in and tolerated lynching in the United States.

While lynching is rare today in the United States, its legacy, like that of antimiscegenation, naturalization law, and immigration policy, continues to shape relationships, neighborhoods, schools, and communities. The symbolic power of a noose hanging from a tree remains strong, the message is clear, and the fear evoked and power asserted is palpable. What is less understood about the symbolism of the noose is its message regarding white Americans. Just as the swastika in light of the history of Nazis during WWII represents failed humanity for Christian Germans, the noose in light of U.S. history represents failed humanity on the part of white Americans.

Let's return to a consideration of gang violence today and your responses to Nazi Germany. How have you responded to killings that are a result of gang violence? What have you said about gang members who engage in these killings? I have heard many responses, including: "What is wrong with them?" "They have no values." "How could anyone treat life with such disregard?" When you learned about the atrocities of the Nazis during World War II did you wonder, "How could those SS officers and soldiers treat another human being like garbage to be disposed?" Have you wondered, "What happened to those soldiers?" These are not uncommon. Notice that there is a presumption in these comments: that full humanity implies a value of life and basic human dignity to be afforded all humanity. These comments also point to the recognition of a problem, a human defect, when one group of humans renders another group subhuman and proceeds to engage in activities and actions that kill.

The meanings that have been assigned to white people, along side those that have been assigned to nonwhites in the U.S., create the conditions for dehumanization and death. The meanings and consequence of whiteness explored in the preceding pages reveal that white people have been materially advantaged and nonwhites materially disadvantaged. In addition, they reveal a diminished humanity by virtue of whiteness. As a result, there is a very real, very tangible reason for white people to work to dismantle whiteness – reclaiming one's humanity.

The Legacy

How is the history of lynching relevant to this historical moment? It is relevant because it shows literally, in the faces of white people, the complete disregard for another human being. While it would be nice to shove that history aside and claim that such disregard is an artifact of the past, there is evidence to suggest otherwise. While the disregard of humanity might be less dramatic than a charred and mutilated body, it is nonetheless evident in the degree to which most white people are unaffected and complacent in the midst of severe harms that nonwhite communities endure. When significant harms become white people's harms, this country takes action. Again, evidence of defective humanity emerges.

If white men constituted 13.6 percent of the U.S. population while whites constituted 39.4 percent of the total prison population, there would be cries that something is foul. If white men were incarcerated at the rate of 4,347 inmates per 100,000 U.S. residents of the same race and gender there would be a public outcry. There would be claims that such figures reveal a social problem, a problem not with white men but with social structures and forces, with the organization of society, with opportunities and pay scales. In light of the fact that numerous prison populations are rendered free labor, there would be outcries that white men are being rendered slave labor to capitalists producing lingerie and sportswear. These numbers of white people behind bars would simply not be tolerated. Why are they tolerated when the numbers reflect black men in the U.S. today?[92]

If white people had to walk around with papers to ensure their freedom in the event that they are suspected of being undocumented, white people would be enraged. There would be outcries that such practices are akin to the black codes in the south following the Civil War and the practices of apartheid South Africa. Why are white people not outraged by the proposal of such practices applied to Hispanic persons in the U.S. today?

If large numbers of white people were stripped of their title to land, harassed, and some lynched by a paramilitary group, white people would never tolerate a professional sports team being named after the group. Why is it okay when that was the experience of Mexicans at the hands, guns and ropes of the Texas Rangers?[93] If the infant mortality rate of white babies were 2.5 times that of another segment of the American population, white people would claim there is a health care crisis. Why are white people not outraged that these numbers reflect the reality for members of native tribes in the U.S. today?[94]

These practices, numbers, and situations are both a legacy and manifestation of white supremacy. Just as the history of lynching exposes human deficiency exhibited by white Americans, so too do these current facts. How can U.S. culture and society be altered when the roots of white supremacy are foundational as a matter of history and law? How can a group of people invented in part through the assertion that they are more deserving of rights and privileges than others be transformed? Is it possible to take something conceived out of superiority and deployed as a wedge between American laborers, and make it humane and fair?

There is no ready answer to these questions. What is clear is that whiteness must be examined and explored. Its impact must be brought into view and exposed as a specific place within the larger framework of racial constructs within the U.S. Ultimately, this project of transforming whiteness begins with you and me. Through the work of self-examination, historical awareness, and cultural critique with an eye toward identifying and unpacking the workings of whiteness, U.S. society will be transformed. Such a process is what I call *white awareness.* White awareness is necessary on the part of those labeled white and those labeled not white. Whether the transformation will be significant enough to shatter the link between whiteness and superiority remains to be seen. Because some of the primary functions of whiteness today are made possible through its invisibility, exposing and objectifying it to analysis reflects a dramatic break from current conceptualizations of race. Such an effort will also challenge at least one of the ways the racial hierarchy that most privileges whites becomes so easily embedded within institutions. What is certain is that white awareness is a critical component to movement in the direction of greater equality and less white supremacy in the U.S.

The good news here is that this is the one place I have some control in the world – me, my interpretations, my perceptions, my compassion, my humanity. The challenge of course is that I am a product of the culture and society within which I have grown up and live, and this culture and society promotes the supremacy of white people over racial others. Even in the face of such monumental forces, the potential and capacities of a person can be great. Personal transformation is first and foremost.

I am not a widget stamped out by a culturally fabricated sheet of metal that produces an identical product with each press of the stamp. Humans have agency. In other words, each person makes choices. Granted, those choices are made within a historical and cultural context that makes it appear as if only a relatively small range of choices are possible. Similarly, while my perceptions are shaped by life experience, I am not a prisoner to them. The fact that I can identify, examine, analyze and critique them and the life experience that has significantly shaped them renders them change-able. I have the power to reject cultural messages that dehumanize by overvaluation and undervaluation. While my personal choices may not transform systems and institutions in any immediate way, they can radically transform.relationships and ways of being by disclosing and disrupting white supremacy.

Throughout this book I have named the roots and effects of the invention of white people as "white supremacy." I have done this despite knowing that the current political environment much prefers the terminology of "white privilege." While the terminology of white privilege is useful by helping to diminish resistance and defensiveness, it is critical to remember that but for white supremacy, white privilege does not exist. While it may be difficult to face white supremacy within our institutions, history, and ourselves, it is a necessary for that truth to be named if it is to be confronted and dismantled.

I have learned quite a bit about race and whiteness, and this helps me to put a check on my enactments of white supremacy. Still, I inflict harm often. Every time I enact white supremacy I shore it up and simultaneously degrade those excluded from its boundaries. Despite this truth, I wake up each day and choose to engage my whiteness and that of the institutions and communities in which I work and live. I am very much on the journey of white awareness. I try not to beat myself up, even while I try to repair where I have inflicted harm. I try to find areas of life that are manageable, to make a change that reaches beyond interpersonal interactions. This book is such an effort. Though, truth be told, there is nothing more powerful than those moments when I have been able to release my hold on supremacy and really let myself experience the humanity of my neighbor. It is in those moments that I have a glimpse of a fuller humanity to which I aspire. I wish you many.

Bibliography

Acuna, Rodolfo F. (2007) *Occupied America: A History of Chicanos.* 6th ed. New York: Pearson.

Allen, Theodore W. (1997) *The Invention of the White Race: The Origin of Racial Oppression in Anglo-America,* Vol.2, London: Verso.

Basch, Norma (1982). *In the Eyes of the Law: Women, Marriage, and Property in Nineteenth-Century.* New York: Cornell University Press.

Bardaglio, Peter W. (1995). *Reconstructing the Household: Families, Sex, and the Nineteenth-Century South.* Chapel Hill, NC: University of North Carolina Press.

Battalora, Jacqueline (1999). Toward a critical white racial ethics: Constructions of whiteness in antimiscegenation law. *Ph.D. dissertation,* Northwestern University.

Bell, Horace (1930). *On the Old West Coast.* New York: Morrow.

Becker, Howard (1963). *Outsiders: Studies in the Sociology of Deviance.* New York: Free Press.

Bevans, Charles I., ed. (1972). *Treaties and Other International Agreements of the United States of America,* 1776-1949, vol. 9. Washington D.C.: Department of State.

Blood, Robert O., Jr. & Donald M. Wolfe (1960). *Husbands & Wives: The Dynamics of Married Living.* Glencoe, Illinois: Free Press.

Bose, Christine E. (1987). "Dual Spheres." In *Analysing Gender,* ed. B. Hess and M. Ferree, (Newbury Park, Calif.: Sage), 267-85.

Brandwein, Pamela (1999). *Reconstructing Reconstruction: The Supreme Court and the Production of Historical Truth.* Chapel Hill: Duke University Press.

Breene, Thomas K. and Keith Innes (1980). *Myne Owne Ground.* Oxford: Oxford University Press.

Bynum, Victoria (1992). *Unruly Women: The Politics of Social and Sexual Control in the Old South.* Chapel Hill, NC: University of North Carolina Press.

Camarillo, Albert (1979). *Chicanos in a Changing Society.* Cambridge, Mass.: Harvard University Press.

Carrigan, William D. and Clive Webb (2003) "The Lynching of Persons of Mexican Origin or Descent in the United States, 1848 To 1928," *Journal of Social History* 37.2.

Castillo (1990). *The Treaty of Guadalupe Hidalgo: A Legacy of Conflict.* Norman, Oklahoma: University of Oklahoma Press.

Collins, Patricia Hill (1998). "It's All in the Family: Intersections of Gender, Race, and Nation," *Hypatia* vol. 13, no. 3 (summer).

Chan, Sucheng (1991). *Asian Americans: An Interpretive History.* Boston: Twayne Publishers.

Crenshaw, Kimberle (1991). Mapping the Margins: Intersectionality, Identity Politics, and Violence against Women of Color, *Stanford L. Rev.*, Vol. 43, No. 6., pp. 1241-1299.

Degler, Carl N. (1960). Out of Our Past: The Forces that Shaped Modern America, 2nd ed. New York: Harper & Row.

Delaney, David (1998). *Race. Place, and the Law, 1836-1948.* Austin: University of Texas Press.

D'Emilio, John & Estelle B. Freedman (1988). *Intimate Matters: A History of Sexuality in America.* New York: Harper & Row.

Deutsch, Sarah (1987). *No Separate Refuge: Culture, Class, and Gender on an Anglo-Hispanic Frontier in the American Southwest, 1880-1940.* New York: Oxford University Press.

Dysart, Jane (1976). "Mexican Women in San Antonio, 1830-1860: The Assimilation Process," *The Western Historical Quarterly* 7 (October).

Edwards, Laura (1997). *Gendered Strife and Confusion: The Political Culture of Reconstruction.* Urbana, IL: University of Illinois.

Eric Foner (1988). *Reconstruction: America's Unfinished Revolution 1963-1877.* New York: Harper & Row.

Fields, Barbara (1981). Ideology and Race in American History, in J. Morgan Kousser and James M. McPherson, eds, Region, Race, and Reconstruction, New York: Oxford University Press.

Fowler, David. H. (1963). Northern Attitudes Towards Interracial Marriage: A Study of Legislation and Public Opinion in the Middle Atlantic and the States of the Old Northwest. *Ph.D. Dissertation*, Yale University.

Fredrickson, George M. (1971). Toward a Social Interpretation of the Development of American Racism. In *Key Issues in the Afro-American Experience*, vol 1, eds. N.I. Huggins, M. Kilson, and D.M. Fox. 240-252. New York: Harcourt Brace Jovanovich.

_____. (1981) White Supremacy. New York: Oxford University Press.

Getman, Karen A. (1984). Sexual Control in the Slaveholding South: The Implementation and Maintenance of a Racial Caste System, 7 *Harv. Women's L.J.* 115.

Giddens, Anthony. (1976). *New Rules of Sociological Method*, London: Hutchinson.

_____. (1984). *The Constitution of Society: Outline of the Theory of Structuration*, Cambridge: Polity Press.

Glenn, Evelyn Nakano (2002) *Unequal Freedom: How Race and Gender Shaped American Citizenship and Labor*. Cambridge, Massachusetts: Harvard University Press.

Gordon, Charles (1945). The Racial Barrier to American Citizenship, 93 U. PA. L. Rev. 237.

Griswold, Robert L. (1993). *Fatherhood in America: A History*. New York: Basic.

Guttentag, Marcia & Paul F. Secord (1983). *Too Many Women? The sex ratio question*. Beverly Hills: Sage.

Handlin, Oscar and Mary Handlin (1950). The Origins of the Southern Slave System, William and Mary Quarterly, 3rd ser., VII. 199-222.

Higham, John (1955). *Strangers in the Land: Patterns of American Nativism 1860-1925*, 2nd ed. New Brunswick, NY: Rutgers University Press.

Jacobson, Mathew Fry (1998). *Whiteness of a Different Color: European Immigrants and the Alchemy of Race*. Cambridge, Mass.: Harvard University Press.

Jordan, Winthrop D. (1968). *White Over Black: American Attitudes Toward the Negro, 1550-1812*. Baltimore: Penguin.

Kelman, Mark (1987) *A Guide to Critical Legal Studies*. Cambridge MA: Harvard University Press.

Lauber, Almon W. [1913] (1970). *Indian Slavery in Colonial Times within the Present Limits of the United States*. Williamstown, MA: Corner House Publishers.

Lee, Erika. (2003). *At America's Gates: Chinese Immigration during the Exclusion Era*. Chapel Hill: University of North Caroline Press.

Lopez, Ian F. Haney (1996). *White By Law: The Legal Construction of Race*. New York: New York University Press.

Lubiano, Wahneema (1990). Black Ladies, Welfare Queens, and State Minstrels: Ideological War by Narrative Means. Toni Morrison ed., *Racing Justice, Engendering Power*. New York: Pantheon.

Marshall, T.H. (1964). "Citizenship and Social Class," in *Class, Citizenship and Social Development*. New York: Doubleday.

Massey, Douglas S. and Nancy A. Denton (1990). *American Apartheid: Segregation and the Making of the Underclass*. Cambridge, Mass.: Harvard University Press 30-35

Miller, David Hunt (1937). *Treaties and Other International Acts of the United States of America*, vol. 5. Washington, D.C.: Government Printing Office.

Miller, Kirby (1985). *Emigrants and Exiles: Ireland and the Irish Exodus to North America*. New York: Oxford University Press.

Miller, Seumas, "Social Institutions", *The Stanford Encyclopedia of Philosophy (Spring 2011 Edition)*, Edward N. Zalta (ed.), http://plato.stanford.edu/archives/spr2011/entries/social-institutions/

Mirande, Alfredo (1985). *The Chicano Experience: An Alternative Perspective*. South Bend, Indiana: University of Notre Dame Press.

Montgomery, David (1980). "The Irish and the American Labor Movement," in David Doyle, Owen Dudley Edwards, and Cumann

Merriman, eds, *America and Ireland, 1776-1976*, Westport, Conn.: Greenwood Press.

Morgan, Philip D. (1998). *Slave Counterpoint: Black Culture in the 18th Century Chesapeake & Lowcountry*. Chapel Hill: University of North Carolina Press.

Morgan, Edmond S. (1975). *American Slavery, American Freedom*. New York: W.W. Norton.

Nash, Gary B. (1992). *Red, White, and Black: The Peoples of Early America*. 3rd ed. Englewood Cliffs, NJ: Prentice-Hall.

Omi, Michael & Howard Winant (1994). *Racial Formations in the United States: From the 1960s to the 1990s*. 2nd ed. New York: Routledge.

Ortis, Robert (1992). "The Religious Boundaries of an Inbetween People: Street *Feste* and the Problem of the Dark-Skinned 'Other' in Italian Harlem, 1920-1990," *American Quarterly* 44 (September).

Pieterse, Jan Nederveen (1992). *White On Black: Images of Africa and Blacks in Western Popular Culture*. New Haven, CT: Yale University Press.

Parent, Anthony S., Jr. (2003). *Foul Means: The Formation of Slave Society in Virginia, 1660-1740*. Chapel Hill: University of North Carolina Press.

Reisler, Mark (1976). *By the Sweat of Their Brow: Mexican Immigration Labor in the United States, 1900-1940*. Westport, Conn.: Greenwood Press.

Richardson, Laurel (2008). "Gender Stereotyping in the English Language." In K. E. Rosenblum and T. C. Travis, eds., *The Meaning of Difference: American Constructions of Race, Sex and Gender, Social Class, Sexual Orientation, and Disability*, 5th ed. New York: McGraw-Hill.

Roediger, David R. (1991). *The Wages of Whiteness: Race and the Making of the American Working Class*. London: Verso.

_____ (2005). *Working Toward Whiteness: How America's Immigrants Became White*. New York: Basic Books.

Root, Maria P. (2001). *Love's Revolution: Interracial Marriage*. Philadelphia, PA: Temple University.

Rowe, G.E. (1989). Black Offenders, Criminal Courts and Philadelphia Society in the Late Eighteenth Century, *Journal of Social History* 22 (Summer).

Ruether, Rosemary Radford (2009). *Christianity and Social Systems: Historical Constructions and Ethical Challenges*. Lanham, MD: Rowman & Littlefield Publishers.

Salmon, Marylynn. (1979). Equality or Submersion? Feme Covert Status in Early Pennsylvania. In Carol Ruth Berkin and Mary Beth Norton. (eds.) *Women of America: A History*. Boston: Houghton Mifflin.

Saxton, Alexander (1990). *The Rise and Fall of the White Republic: Class Politics and Mass Culture in Nineteenth-Century America*. London: Verso Books.

Shakespeare, William (1604). The Tragedy of Othello, The Moor of Venice. In *Literature: An introduction to fiction, Poetry, and Drama*. 4th ed., ed. X. J. Kennedy. Boston: Little Brown and Company.

Smedley, Audrey (2007). *Race in North America: Origin and Evolution of a Worldview*. 3rd ed. Boulder, CO: Westview Press.

Smith, Abbot E. (1947). *Colonists in Bondage: White Servitude and Convict Labor in America, 1607-1776*. Chapel Hill: University of North Carolina Press.

Sickels, Robert J. (1972). *Race, Marriage, and the Law*. Albuquerque, NM: University of New Mexico.

Spickard, Paul R. (1989). *Mixed Blood: Intermarriage and Ethnic Identity in Twentieth-Century America*. Madison: University of Wisconsin Press.

Spruill, Julia Cherry (1998). *Women's Life and Work in the Southern Colonies*. New York: W.W. Norton & Company.

Stanly, Julia P. (1977) "Paradigmatic Woman: The Prostitute." In D.L. Shores, ed., *Papers in Language Variation*. Birmingham: University of Alabama Press.

Star, Susan Leigh (1988). Introduction: "The Sociology of Science and Technology" (Special Issue), 35 *Social Problems* 3.

_____ (1989). *Regions of the Mind: Brain Research and the Quest for Scientific Certainty*. Stanford, CA: Stanford University Press.

Stone, Lawrence. (1977). *The Family Sex, and Marriage in England, 1500-1800*. London: Weidenfeld & Nicolson.

Turner, Jonathan. (1997). *The Institutional Order*, New York: Longman.

U.S. Bureau of Justice Statistics. (June 2010). Prison inmates for 2010 Statistical Tables.

U.S. Census Bureau. (2010). Overview of Race and Hispanic Origin: 2010 Census Briefs.

Wells, Robert V. (1975). *The population of the British colonies in America before 1776*. Princeton, NJ: Princeton University Press.

Williams, Glanville, L. (1947). The Legal Unity of Husband and Wife. 10 *Mod. L. Rev.* 16.

Williams, Patricia. (1990). Metro Broadcasting v. FCC. 104 *Harv. L.Rev.* 525.

Cases

Dred Scott v. Sandford, 60 U.S. (19 How.) 393 (1857).

In re Knight, 171 F. 299, 300 (E.D.N.Y. 1909)

Loving v. Virginia, 388 U.S. 1, 3 (1967).

Perez v. Sharp, 32 Cal.2d 711, 198 P2d 17 (*sub. nom. Perez v. Lippord*) (1948).

Plessy v. Ferguson, 163 U.S. 537 (1896).

In re Rodriguez, 81 F. 337 (W.D. Tex. 1897).

U.S. v. Thind, 261 U.S. 204 (1923).

Statutes

Act of March 26, 1790, ch.3, Stat. 103.

Act of March 2, 1907, ch. 2534, § 3, 34 Stat. 1228.

Act of Sept. 22, 1922, ch. 411, § 2, 42 Stat. 1021.

Act of March 3, 1931, ch. 442, § 4(a), 46 Stat. 1511.

Chinese Exclusion Act, ch. 126, 22 Stat. 58 (1882).

Immigration Act of 1924, ch. 190 §13(c), 43 Stat. 162.

Immigration and Naturalization Act of 1952, § 311, ch. 2, 66 Stat. 239 (codified as amendment at 8 U.S.C. § 1422 [1988]).

Brown, W.H. et. al eds., 1883-1956. *Archives of Maryland*, __vols.

Arch. Md. 1:97

Arch. Md. 1: 526-527

Arch. Md. 1: 533

Arch. Md. 2: 272

Arch. Md. 7: 203-205

Arch. Md. 13: 546-549

Hening, William W. comp. 1809-1823. *The Statutes at Large: Being A Collection of All the Laws of Virginia.* (1619-1792). 13 vols. Richmond, Virginia: Published by Act of the General Assembly of Virginia and printed by and for Samuel Pleasants Jr., printer to the commonwealth.

Hening 1: 252-253

Hening 2: 170

Hening 2: 267

Hening 2:280-281

Hening 3: 74

Hening 3: 86-88

Hening 3: 103

Hening 3: 139

Hening 3: 298

Hening 3: 361

Hening 3: 447-62

Hening 3: 453-54

Hening 3: 459-60

Hening 4: 119

Hening 4: 126-34

Hening 4: 327

Hening 4: 352

Hurd, (1714). *Law of Freedom and Bondage*, 1:266, *citing Acts and Laws Passed by the General Court or Assembly of His Majesty's Province of New Hampshire in New England.* Boston: B. Green, 1726.

Immigration and Nationality Act of 1952 § 101 (a)(23), 66 Stat. 169 (codified as amended at 8 U.S.C. § 1101[a][23][1988]).

Nevill, Samuel. comp. 1752. *The Acts of the General Assembly of the Province of New Jersey*, 2 vols. Philadelphia: Printed by William Bradford, printed for province of New Jersey.

NOTES

1   Kimberle Crenshaw coined the term intersectionalty (1991). Mapping the Margins: Intersectionality, Identity Politics, and Violence against Women of Color, *Stanford L. Rev.*, Vol. 43, No. 6., pp. 1241-1299.

2   Prior to graduate studies, I had no formal training in sociology except for that provided through a friend, sociologist and political scientist, Pamela Brandwein. Brandwein introduced me to the sociology of science through her use of it in her research exploring the Fairman-Croskey debate over the incorporation of the Fourteenth Amendment. I am indebted to her for making the introduction and for revealing its value through her own research and writing. Any error or limitation in the application of tools from the sociology of science is solely my own. See, Brandwein, Pamela (1999). *Reconstructing Reconstruction: The Supreme Court and the Production of Historical Truth.* Chapel Hill: Duke University Press.

3   The status of Middle Eastern people in the U.S. today who are officially classified as white but who are not treated as such in and through daily interactions constitute a contemporary example.

4   There is dispute about the time period wherein the "white race" was created. Barbara Fields (1982) locates the origin of the modern concept of race in the nineteenth century and David Goldberg (2002) locates it in the fifteenth century, while Theodore Allen (1997) locates it at the conclusion of the seventeenth and start of the eighteenth century. I find Allen most persuasive and firmly backed by legal enactments.

5   The company was created by a charter from King James I to Richard Hakluyt and others in 1606 (Morgan 1975: 84; 44-45).

6   A raid by a native tribe in 1622 killed 347 settlers, while 3,000 were killed by other means (Morgan 1975: 101). An investigation

revealed that ship captains interested in collecting the transportation fee "overloaded ships with passengers and dumped the survivors ashore in Virginia half dead with scurvy" (Ibid). There was some shortage of food between 1618 and 1624 but Morgan concludes that the problem was not whether there were adequate supplies, but rather who held them and could afford them (Ibid. at105).

7 Allen here cites Wesley Frank Craven, *White, Red, and Black: the Seventeenth-century Virginian* (Charlottesville, 1971; New York, 1977), p. 5, 14-16, 85-86.

8 Historians who have argued that the British arrived upon the shores of North America with antipathy toward black Africans firmly entrenched include Winthrop Jordan 1968, Carl Degler 1959-1960, and Arnold Sio 1964-1965.

9 Virginia passed a fornication law in 1662 that doubled the fine when one party was British and the other African. See, *supra* p. 35.

10 For a detailed explanation of the patriarchal ideals in pre-modern England see, Lawrence Stone (1977). *The Family Sex, and Marriage in England, 1500-1800.* London: Weidenfeld & Nicolson.

11 In 1664, a child's status in Maryland was dependent upon the status of the child's father, consistent with British law. In 1692 in "An Act concerning Negro Slaves" a child's status as free required that both parents be free. It provided that "all children ... born of any Negroes or other Slaves within this Province shall be Slaves to all intents and purposes as their parents were for the Terme of their naturall Liues." *(Arch. Md.* 1692, 13:546-549).

12 The word "miscegenation" was coined by David Goodman Croly in an anonymous pamphlet published in New York by H. Dexter, Hamilton, and Co., 1863. The pamphlet was an attempt by Democrats David Croly and George Wakeman to attribute favorable views on "racial mixing" to Republicans, thereby promoting support for the Democratic candidate for president (Sickels 1972).

13 Academics most often refer to antimiscegenation law as laws that imposed racial restrictions upon marriage. Such a description is misleading because it presents a level racial playing field, as if

all groups understood as racially distinct, faced restrictions. This was not the case. Antimiscegenation law only restricted those understood prior to 1681 as "British and other freeborns" and after 1681 as "whites" from marrying a variety of "others," including blacks, Asians, Indians and others, depending upon the population within the region. Even though a person referenced in the law as an "Indian" was understood as racially distinct from a person from China, such a marriage was not prohibited. It was only where a party was understood to be white that restrictions were imposed under antimiscegenation law.

14 The excavation of the sunken slave ship called the *Henrietta Marie* is particularly illuminating. The web site www.melfisher.org/exhibitions/henriettamarrie/research.htm offers detailed information about the grueling conditions faced by Africans transported across the Atlantic.

15 Jordan, citing "Decisions of the General Court," *Virginia Magazine of History and Biography*, 5 (1898), 236-37.

16 Some historians have suggested that antimiscegenation laws, specifically those concerning native tribal members, may have had motivations other than antipathy toward those with physical differences from the English (Frederickson 1981; Nash 1992).

17 Ian Haney Lopez' study of naturalization law prerequisite cases reveals that prior to 1923, there were competing approaches utilized by courts to determine who is white, one relying on science and the other on common knowledge (1996). Determining who was white was critical to those born outside the U.S. who sought citizenship, because U.S. naturalization law required that one be white in order to naturalize as a citizen (Act of March 26, 1790, ch.3, Stat. 103). The conflict was settled by the U.S. Supreme Court in, U.S. v. Thind, in favor of "common knowledge" (261 U.S. 204 (1923)).

18 This is reflected in legislation passed by the Maryland Assembly, but vetoed by the proprietor, that would have required a woman to marry within seven years of her arrival in the colony or else lose her land or the ability to pass it on to her heirs upon her death. While this legislation was never enacted, it reveals the pressures the men in control of community law were willing to place upon

women to marry. It also reveals the correlation between gender and control over the creation of community standards and relational behavior in the colonial North American context (Guttentag & Secord 1983: 116 (citing Spruill, op. cit., 1938)).

19 It has been shown across time and cultures that when women are scarce relative to men, a protective morality is created by men with structural power "that favors monogamy for women, limits their interactions with men, and shapes female roles in traditional domestic relations" (Guttentag & Secord 1983: 231). Constraints upon women's interactions are imposed by men who possess structural power within the culture. In other words, they are imposed by men who control the creation and enforcement of law, the economy, and most other powerful cultural institutions.

20 Allen cites at length from the a letter of objection issued by Richard West, the Attorney General in England who was charged with reviewing enactments from the British colonies to determine whether they should be approved or rejected as prejudicial or contradictory to the laws of England. In opposing a Virginia colony enactment that prohibited a free Negro, mulatto or Indian from voting at an election of burgesses, West stated, in part, "I cannot see why one freeman should be used worse than another, merely upon account his complexion...." (241 citing George Chalmers, comp. and ed., *Opinions of Eminent Lawyers on Various Points of English Jurisprudence chiefly concerning the Colonies, Fisheries, and Commerce*, 2 vols. (London, 1814; Burt Franklin Reprint, 1971, from the original edition in the Brooklyn Public Library) 2:113-14.

21 I encourage instructors or group facilitators to implement this exercise prior to assigning Chapter 2. I always inform my department chair and the dean of the College of Arts and Sciences about the exercise in which I am engaging my students. In the event that students exercise a voice of concern regarding injustice to the "authorities," this communication helps foster support and understanding within the department and school. I also let these university authority figures know the date at which students will know that they were participating in an exercise and that the grades given in the unequal grading scheme will be discarded, counting instead as "complete" or "incomplete" course work.

22 Most generally, interactionism is concerned with individuals and how they act within society. James Parker and George Herbert Mead were significant to the development of this theoretical tradition.

23 An exception was carved out for free persons of African descent who were "householders" or who lived on a "frontier plantation" and could secure a license from the justice of the peace. If these conditions were met, the law allowed for possession of one gun and the powder and shot it required (Henning 1723, 4:130).

24 "Whiteness" reflects more than those understood to fall within the category "white." It is meant to capture the ideological and social structural components that have been built along side and in conjunction with the invention of "white" people. This will be discussed further in this chapter.

25 By far the greatest burden of violating the Maryland law fell upon free black men and the children of a prohibited couple. A free black man who married a white woman was prescribed the harshest punishment – service to the parish for life, the loss of his freedom. Any child born to a white woman in violation of the law was required to serve the parish until the age of twenty-one (*Arch. Md.* 13: 546-549).

26 In the 1660s, women and children who were native tribal members were specified as the "booty" for the militiamen who attacked specific northern tribes (Allen 1997: 207).

27 I derive "moral entrepreneur" from Howard Becker (1963: 149-50).

28 Delaware did not pass an antimiscegenation law that punished "white" and "nonwhite" persons who married. Delaware did pass numerous laws addressing non-marital liaisons between "white" people and African or mulatto persons. New Jersey, New Hampshire, and Connecticut never passed antimiscegenation laws. This is not to say that the laws of these colonies were free of white supremacism and its accompanying racial hierarchy. The enforcement of the meanings of "white" and "nonwhite" came through numerous laws. A New Jersey law described free people of African descent as "idle" and "slothful" (Hurd 1713, 1:284). New Hampshire relied upon derogatory stereotypes of the American Indian servant or slave (Hurd 1714, 1:266).

29　There are many important scholars who have examined ideology and sharpened and differentiated the ideological concept. Some examples include: Karl Marx' conceptualization of superstructure within his model of society. In this model, the base reflects relations of production and the superstructure reflects dominant ideology. George Walford and Harold Walsby explore the relationship between ideology and social systems under the heading *systematic ideology*.

30　Lynching is an extrajudicial execution of a person(s) carried out by a number of people usually a large group or a mob. In other words, it is an execution conducted outside of any judicial or criminal justice process.

31　Cheryl Harris argues that whiteness has become a form of property with material value that those who hold the label can utilize and deploy for their benefit (1993).

32　Emphasis in original.

33　Ian F. Haney Lopez' study of Naturalization law prerequisite cases reveals that, prior to 1923, there were competing approaches utilized by courts to determine who is "white," one relying on science and the other on common knowledge (1996: 79-80). Determining who was "white" was critical to these cases because U.S. naturalization law required that one be *white* in order to Naturalize as a citizen (Act of March 26, 1790, ch.3, Stat. 103). The conflict was settled by the U.S. Supreme Court in *U.S. v. Thind*, in favor of "common knowledge" (261 U.S. 204 (1923)).

34　Race, until the early twentieth century, denoted genetically distinct human populations marked by common phenotypic traits (Gordon 1964).

35　For a good review of contemporary biological and genetic claims about the human genome in relation to the concept of "race," see Audrey Smedley, *Race in North America: Origin and evolution of a worldview*, 3rd Ed. (Boulder, Colorado: Westview Press, 2007), 22-35 and Chapter 13.

36　Immigration and Naturalization Act of 1952, § 311, ch. 2, 66 Stat. 239 (codified as amendment at 8 U.S.C. § 1422 [1988].

37　Theodore T. Allen, *The Invention of the White Race*. Vol. 2. (New York: Verso, 1997); Barbara Fields, 'Ideology and Race in

American History,' J. Morgan Kousser and James N. McPherson, eds. *Region, Race and Reconstruction*. (New York: Oxford University Press, 1982).

38 David R. Roediger, *Wages of Whiteness: Race and the Making of the American Working Class* (London:Verso, 1991, 1992, 1993), 54.

39 Roediger, *Wages of Whiteness*, 57.

40 Eric Foner, *Reconstruction: America's Unfinished Revolution 1963-1877* (New York: Harper & Row, 1988) provides a rich description of this extraordinary period in U.S. history.

41 In *Plessy*, the U.S. Supreme Court ruled that the U.S. Constitution allowed the "separate but equal" treatment of black and white people, providing the legal support for American apartheid. David Delaney, *Race. Place, and the Law, 1836-1948* (Austin: University of Texas Press, 1998) 125-178; Douglas S. Massey and Nancy A. Denton, *American Apartheid: Segregation and the Making of the Underclass* (Cambridge, Mass.: Harvard University Press, 1993) 30-35.

42 Evelyn Nakano Glenn, *Unequal Freedom: How Race and Gender Shaped American Citizenship and Labor* (Cambridge, Mass.: Harvard University Press, 2002) 193, 203-205; 203. Parenthetical added for clarification.

43 Smedley, *Race in North America*, 276.

44 Abraham Lincoln, 'Third Annual Message,' 8 December 1863, quoted in Alexander Saxton, *The Rise and Fall of the White Republic: Class Politics and Mass Culture in Nineteenth-Century America* (London: Verso, 1990) 250.

45 Hiroshi Motmoura. Americans in Waiting: The Lost Story of Immigration and Citizenship in the United States. New York: Oxford University Press, 2006) 19.

46 John Higham. Strangers in the Land: Patterns of American Nativism 1860-1925, 2nd ed. (New Brunswick, NY: Rutgers University Press, 1955) 10-15; Saxton, White Republic, 229; Matthew Fry Jacobson. Whiteness of a Different Color: European Immigrants and the Alchemy of Race. (Cambridge, Mass.: Harvard University Press, 1998).

47 Christine E. Bose. Dual Spheres. In *Analysing Gender*, B. Hess and M. Ferree, eds., 267-85. (Newbury Park, Calif.: Sage, 1987),

267-85; Robert L. Griswold. *Fatherhood in America: A History.* (New York: Basic, 1993).

48 Glenn, *Unequal Freedom,* 36-39; 82-84.

49 Glenn, *Unequal Freedom,* 154, 196-197.

50 In response to complaints that American gold was being filtered to such places as China, Mexico, South America, and Australia, the California legislature passed the Foreign Miner's Tax of 1850 that required those who were not native or naturalized citizens to pay $20 a month for a license to mine. This incredible fee quickly gave rise to protest and violence. Within one year the tax was repealed and then reinstated in 1852, at the rate of $4.00 a month.

51 Saxton, *White Republic,* 297.

52 Immigration Act of 1924, ch. 190 §13(c), 43 Stat. 162.

53 Sucheng Chan, *Asian Americans: An Interpretive History* (Boston: Twayne Publishers, 1991).

54 Smedley, *Race in North America,* 278; Immigration Act of 1924, ch. 190 §13(c), 43 Stat. 162.

55 Erika Lee. At America's Gates: Chinese Immigration during the Exclusion Era. (Chapel Hill: University of North Caroline Press, 2003), 35-36.

56 John Higham, *Strangers in the Land: Patterns of American Nativism, 1860-1925* (New York, 1974), 169; Robert Ortis, "The Religious Boundaries of an Inbetween People: Street *Feste* and the Problem of the Dark-Skinned 'Other' in Italian Harlem, 1920-1990," *American Quarterly* 44 (September 1992); David Roediger. *Working Toward Whiteness: How America's Immigrants Became White* (New York: Basic Books, 2005), 12.

57 Rodolfo F. Acuna. *Occupied America: A History of Chicanos,* 6th ed. (New York: Pearson, 2007), 36-37.

58 Richard Griswold del Castillo. *The Treaty of Guadalupe Hidalgo: A Legacy of Conflict.* (Norman, Oklahoma: University of Oklahoma Press, 1990), 3-4. Acuna. *Occupied America,* 44.

59 Acuna. *Occupied America,* 36-37; Castillo. *The Treaty of Guadalupe Hidalgo.* 62-63.

60 Charles I. Bevans, ed., *Treaties and Other International Agreements of the United States of America,* 1776-1949, vol. 9 (Washington D.C.: Department of State, 1972), 798.

61 Ibid. at 797-98.

62 Acuna. *Occupied America,* 49-50, citing Antonio de la Pena y Reyes, Algunos Documentos Sobre el Tratado de Guadalupe-Hidalgo (Mexico, D.F.: Sec de Rel. Ext., 1930), 159. quoted in Richard Gonzales, "Commentary on the Treaty of Guadalupe Hidalgo," in Feliciano Rivera, A Mexican American Source Book (Menlo Park, Cal.: Educational Consulting Associates, 1970), 185.

63 Albert Camarillo, *Chicanos in a Changing Society* (Cambridge, Mass.: Harvard University Press, 1979) 114-16; Sarah Deutsch, *No Separate Refuge: Culture, Class, and Gender on an Anglo-Hispanic Frontier in the American Southwest, 1880-1940* (New York: Oxford University Press, 1987), 20.

64 Castillo, *The Treaty of Guadalupe Hidalgo,* 68-80; Alfredo Mirande, *The Chicano Experience: An Alternative Perspective* (South Bend, Indiana: University of Notre Dame Press, 1985) 16-23; William D. Carrigan and Clive Webb, "The Lynching of Persons of Mexican Origin or Descent in the United States, 1848 To 1928," *Journal of Social History* 37.2 (Winter 2003): 415.

65 Mark Reisler, *By the Sweat of Their Brow: Mexican Immigration Labor in the United States, 1900-1940* (Westport, Conn.: Greenwood Press, 1976), 136.

66 Section 394 of the Civil Practice Act of the State of California provided, "No Indian or Negro shall be allowed to testify as a witness in any action in which a White person is a party." Section 14 of that state's Criminal Code provided, "No Black, or Mulatto person, or Indian shall be allowed to give evidence in favor of, or against a White man." The result of these statutes were drawn upon by the California Supreme Court in the 1854 case, *People v. Hall,* held that the words, Indian, Negro, Black and White, are generic terms, designating race and therefore Chinese and all other people not white, are prohibited from testifying against whites (4 Cal. 399 (1854)).

67 Ibid. at 52, 147, 160-61.

68 Martha Menchaca, *The Mexican Outsiders: A Community History of Marginalization and Discrimination in California* (Austin: University of Texas Press, 1995), 15.

69 Glenn, *Unequal Freedom,* 154, 196-197; Reisler, *Sweat of Their Brow*, 80-81.

70 Paul R. Spickard, *Mixed Blood: Intermarriage and Ethnic Identity in Twentieth-Century America* (Madison: University of Wisconsin Press, 1989), 374-375; Reisler, *Sweat of their Brow*, 135; Acuna. *Occupied America*, 69; Glenn. *Unequal Freedom*, 52.

71 Horace Bell, *On the Old West Coast* (New York: Morrow, 1930), 255-257. Jane Dysart, "Mexican Women in San Antonio, 1830-1860: The Assimilation Process," *The Western Historical Quarterly* 7 (October 1976): 370-71.

72 Today people from the Middle East are, as a matter of official classification, white or Caucasian but receive few of the everyday benefits of whiteness, including the presumption of being American or loyal to the U.S.

73 T.H. Marshall (1964). "Citizenship and Social Class," in Class, Citizenship and Social Development. New York: Doubleday, 78.

74 Miller, Kirby (1985). Emigrants and Exiles: Ireland and the Irish Exodus to North America. New York: Oxford University Press, 193, 198, 318; David Montgomery, "The Irish and the American Labor Movement," in David Doyle, Owen Dudley Edwards, and Cumann Merriman, eds, America and Ireland, 1776-1976, Westport, Conn.: Greenwood Press, 1980, 205.

75 Ignatiev, *How the Irish Became White*, 40-41, citing from a report by a Philadelphia grand jury on living conditions in the Moyamensing district; the report, according to Ignatiev, had attached to it an article entitled "the Mysteries and Miseries of Philadelphia," appearing originally in the *Evening Bulletin*.

76 Saxton, *The Rise and Fall of the White Republic* 59. The economic diversity included slave-based agriculture in the south, manufacturing in the mid-Atlantic and northern states that "tended toward separate constituencies and regional differentiation of class interests. North of the Patomac the process intensified upper-class adhesion to the National Republican thesis; southward it tended to split the upper class into Whig and regionalist (state's rights) factions." 71.

77 *The Rise and Fall of the White Republic*, 60-63, 66

78 Ignatiev, *How the Irish Became White*, 68; Roediger, *Wages of Whiteness*, 140, 144. The claim that the U.S. was perhaps the most

Birth of a White Nation

democratic during this time is based upon the lack of restrictions on the franchise for citizens and upon the relative weakness of the state (i.e., police or armed enforcers of "the peace."

79 Kirby, *Emigrants and Exiles*, 318; Ignatiev, *How the Irish Became White*, 109.

80 Cited by Kerby Miller, unpub. ms., 41.

81 Ignatiev, *How the Irish Became White*, 75; Roediger, *Wages of Whiteness*, 148-49.

82 Roediger, *Wages of Whiteness*, 148. Ignatiev, *How the Irish Became White*, 132. Roediger explains, "Even the wholesale wartime atrocities against Blacks in the 1863 draft riots did not draw any opposition for assembled crowds nor vigorous prosecutions by municipal authorities." 148.

83 Ignatiev, *How the Irish Became White*, 99.

84 *How the Irish Became White*, 112; Roediger, *Wages of Whiteness*, 144-49.

85 For a detailed description of Irish history as a result of British invasion and then rule as a precursor to and model for racial exploitation that grew in the U.S. see, Theodore Allen, *The Invention of the White Race: Racial Oppression and Social Control*, vol. I, (London: Verso, 1994); Ignatiev, *How the Irish Became White*, 13; 30; Roediger, *Wages of Whiteness* 137.

86 Roediger, *Wages of Whiteness* 136; Ignatiev, *How the Irish Became White* 13-14.

87 *How the Irish Became White*, 12, citing Hugh's statement published in *The Liberator* of March 25, 1842.

88 *How the Irish Became White*, 30.

89 Saxton, *The Rise and Fall of the White Republic*, 71.

90 Ignatiev, *How the Irish Became White*, 30.

91 James Allen, ed. (2010). *Without Sanctuary*, San Francisco: Twin Palms, 2010.

92 Prison inmates for 2010 Statistical Tables, U.S. Bureau of Justice Statistics: June 2010; Overview of Race and Hispanic Origin: 2010 Census Briefs. U.S. Census Bureau. According to the US Bureau of Justice Statistics, non-Hispanic blacks made up 39.4% of the total prison and jail population in 2009. According to the 2010 census of the U.S. Census Bureau, Hispanic and non-

Hispanic blacks constitute 13.6% of the total U.S. population. In 2010 Non-Hispanic black males were incarcerated at the rate of 4,347 inmates per 100,000 U.S. residents of the same race and gender. White males were incarcerated at the rate of 678 inmates per 100,000 U.S. residents of the same race and gender. Hispanic males were incarcerated at the rate of 1,755 inmates per 100,000 U.S. residents of the same race and gender.

93 Rodolfo F. Acuna. *Occupied America: A History of Chicagoans.* 6th ed. (New York: Pearson Longman, 2007) 59-61 and 65-66.

94 MF MacDorman, and TJ Mathews. "Understanding racial and ethnic disparities in U.S. infant mortality rates." NCHS Data Brief no. 74. Hayattsville, MD: US Department of Health and Human Services, CDC, National Center for Health Statistics; 2011. The infant mortality rate for American Indian or Alaskan Native Women was 4.59 infant deaths per 1,000 live births. The infant mortality rate for non-Hispanic white women was 2.29 infant deaths per 1,000 live births.